FRYDERYK CHOPIN
WALTZES
published posthumously

Performance Commentary
Source Commentary (abridged)

PERFORMANCE COMMENTARY

Remarks concerning the musical text

The v a r i a n t furnished with the term *ossia* was thus marked in one of the autographs of the *Waltz in A♭*, WN 47; the variants without this designation result from discrepancies in the text among sources or the impossibility of an unequivocal reading of the text.

Minor authentic differences (single notes, ornaments, slurs and ties, accents, pedal signs, etc.) which may be regarded as variants are given in round brackets ( ), editorial additions in square brackets [ ].

Performers with no interest in source-related problems and wishing to rely on a single text without variants are advised to follow the text given on the main staffs, whilst taking account of all markings in brackets.

Chopin's original fingering is marked with slightly larger digits in Roman type, **1 2 3 4 5**, distinct from editorial fingering, which is written in smaller italics, *1 2 3 4 5*.

General problems regarding the interpretation of Chopin's works will be discussed in a separate volume entitled *Introduction to the National Edition*, in the section 'Problems of Performance'.

Abbreviations: R.H. – right hand; L.H. – left hand.

The choice of version

Several of the *Waltzes* contained in the present volume set the pianist the problem of choosing which version to play. This choice may be informed by the following suggestions:

— all the versions included in the main part of the volume (pp. 12-43) may be used in concert performance;

— the versions marked with the letter 'a' are recommended by the editors as those most finely polished by Chopin (see 'Remarks on the *Waltzes* of series B' in the *Source Commentary*);

— the versions included in the *Appendix* primarily illustrate particular issues relating to the sources and are not meant for concert performance;

— the experienced pianist may—should he deem it appropriate to his interpretational conception—incorporate in the version of the whole work that he has chosen different redactions of certain fragments taken from other versions; nevertheless, extreme caution is advised, so as not to disturb the inner logic of the course of the music. Examples of admissible borrowings of this sort are: bar 35 of the *Waltz in B minor*, WN 19 (in performing version 2a, the variant of this motif that appears in version 2b may be used in the R.H.), bar 8 of the *Waltz in A♭*, WN 47 (in the L.H. the harmonic variant of the 3ʳᵈ beat from version 7a may be incorporated into version 7b) and bar 5 of the *Waltz in F minor*, WN 55 (in version 8b the grace note appearing in version 8a may be added in the R.H.).

Pedalling

Pedal markings appear in only some of the *Waltzes* of the present volume and are generally fragmentary. This does not mean, of course, that pedal should be used only where it was marked by Chopin. The authentic pedalling of the *Waltz in A♭*, WN 47—the most precisely marked of the series B *Waltzes* in this respect—and also of the *Waltzes* intended by Chopin for print, leads to the conclusion that passages with a typical, dance accompaniment should generally be played with harmonic pedals, taken at the beginning of each bar. An execution with shorter pedals or without pedal is recommended wherever the bass note at the beginning of the bar is held with the hand or where a change of harmony occurs on the 3ʳᵈ beat. A single pedal may be used for two-bar segments with an identical accompaniment.

1. Waltz in E major, WN 18

p. 12
Bar 9 R.H. The grace note should be played in an anticipated manner, with the third e^2-$g\#^2$ struck simultaneously with the *e* in the L.H.

Bars 23 & 55 R.H. The grace note may be performed in an anticipated manner (before the third a^1-$c\#^2$ struck together with the L.H. chord) or simultaneously with the crotchet a^1 and the L.H. chord:

In both cases the grace note should be lighter than the neighbouring melodic principals b^1 and $c\#^2$.

2. Waltz in B minor, WN 19

2a. Later version

p. 14
Beginning The term *dolente* that appears in one of the sources (see version 2b) is well suited to the character of the opening part of the *Waltz*, regardless of the version.

Bar 24 R.H. Another authentic way of accentuating this bar:

Bar 25 R.H. More stylish is the execution of the variant grace note simultaneously with the 1ˢᵗ crotchet of the L.H.

Bars 27 & 28 R.H. The grace notes should be lighter than the dotted crotchets that follow them. It is less important whether they fall simultaneously with the L.H. crotchets or slightly before them.

p. 15
Bars 58 & 60 R.H. The grace notes e^2 are better taken simultaneously with the L.H. *A♯*.

Bars 65, 67 & analog. R.H. Different fingering:

2b. Earlier version

p. 17
Bars 13 & 45 R.H. The grace note $f\#^2$ sounds more naturally when played in an anticipated manner (see corresponding fragment in version 2a).

3. Waltz in D flat major, WN 20

p. 21
Bars 24 & 48 R.H. Differing fingering:

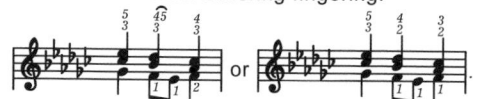

5. Waltz in E minor, WN 29

The grace notes in bars 61-64 & analog. should be played simultaneously with the L.H.; this also applies to the double and triple grace notes in bars 57 & 71 & analog. Such an execution is also recommended in bars 13-15 & analog., whereas the double grace note in bar 11 & analog. may be played either in an anticipated manner or together with the bass note.

6. Waltz in G flat major, WN 42

pp. 28, 30, 32 *Bars 19, 20 & 23* R.H. The grace notes should be played in an anticipated manner.

pp. 29, 31, 33 *Bars 25 & 41* R.H. The grace notes should be played simultaneously with the L.H.

6a. Version in the latest autograph

p. 28 *Anacrusis & Bar 1* R.H. Regardless of the notation, both ornaments should most probably be executed as mordents (∿).

p. 29 *Bar 39* R.H. Execution of the arpeggio with grace note:

A more stylish execution is to strike the first note, gb^1, simultaneously with the L.H. However, in this harmonic context, an anticipated execution is also possible (gb^2 together with the L.H.).

Bar 40 R.H. If arpeggiating the first chord, its bottom note, f^1, should be struck simultaneously with the bass note.

6b. Version in the earlier autograph

p. 31 *Bar 39* R.H. The grace note may be played either in an anticipated manner (before the fifth c^2-gb^2 struck together with the L.H. chord) or simultaneously with the crotchet c^2 and the L.H. chord:

Regardless of the rhythmic solution adopted, the grace note should be lighter than the melodic principal gb^2 that follows it.

6c. Version in the earliest autograph

p. 32 *Anacrusis* R.H. The trill may be executed as a group of 5 notes (♫♫♪) or as a mordent.

p. 33 *Bar 39* R.H. Possibilities for the execution of the grace note—as in the analogous bar of version 6b (see above).

Bar 40 R.H. If arpeggiating the first chord, its bottom note, f^1, should be struck simultaneously with the bass note.

7. Waltz in A flat major, WN 47

pp. 34, 36 *Bar 12 & analog.* R.H. The grace note a^1 is better played simultaneously with the db in the L.H.

7a. Version in the later autograph

p. 34 *Bar 15 & analog.* R.H. In order to avoid the rhythmic deformation of the triplet at the beginning of the bar, the grace note should be played in an anticipated manner.

7b. Version in the earlier autograph

p. 36 *Bars 11, 14 & analog.* R.H. It is not clear whether the variant in bar 11, marked *ossia* by Chopin, indicates that:
— it may be used in place of the main version every time this bar occurs,
— both versions may be used in a single performance of the *Waltz*.
In the latter case, it seems more natural to use the main version first and then introduce the variant to diversify one or more repeats of this bar.
The variant in bar 14 & analog. may be incorporated in a similar way.

8. Waltz in F minor, WN 55

8a. Version in the autograph for Mme Oury

p. 38 *Bars 4 & 12* R.H. The triple grace note should be played in such a way that its first note is struck simultaneously with the bass note.

Bar 20 R.H. Execution of the 3rd beat:

p. 39 *Bar 52* When choosing the variant version, the performer should repeat the whole of the *Waltz* (without the repeat of bars 1-20) and end with the main version of this bar.

8b. Version in the autograph for Mlle Gavard

p. 40 *Bars 4 & 20* R.H. The triple grace note should be played such that its first note falls simultaneously with the corresponding L.H. crotchet (in bar 20 also together with the e^1 of the lower R.H. voice).

9. Waltz in A minor, WN 63

The execution of the double grace notes in such a way that their first note falls simultaneously with the L.H. should be seen as more stylish. However, more important than the moment of striking is the quality of their sound: they should be light and quick, and so their execution in an anticipated manner is also admissible.

Jan Ekier
Paweł Kamiński

SOURCE COMMENTARY /ABRIDGED/

Initial remarks

The present commentary in abridged form presents an assessment of the extent of the authenticity of sources for particular works, sets out the principles behind the editing of the musical text and discusses all the places where the reading or choice of the text causes difficulty. Post-humous editions are taken into account and discussed only where they may have been based on lost autographs or copies thereof. A precise characterisation of the sources, their relations to one another, the justification of the choice of basic sources, a detailed presentation of the differences appearing between them, and also reproductions of characteristic fragments of the different sources are all contained in a separately published *Source Commentary*.

Abbreviations: R.H. – right hand; L.H. – left hand. The sign → indicates a relationship between sources, and should be read as 'and the source(s) based thereon'.

Remarks on the *Waltzes* of series B

Chopin composed *Waltzes* virtually throughout his creative life. In the list of *Unpublished Works* compiled by Chopin's sister, Ludwika Jędrzejewicz, which includes the incipits of twelve waltzes, the year of the composing of the earliest of these waltzes—with the qualification 'Date uncertain'—is given as 1824 (see *Works lost, inaccessible and dubious* at the end of this commentary). The latest of the extant, *Waltz in A minor*, WN 63, belongs to the group of Chopin's very last works. Even those closest to Chopin had difficulties establishing the exact dates of the composing of the *Waltzes* contained in the present volume: in her list, Ludwika altered the dates attributed to *Waltzes* many times, and not all the dates which she ultimately left proved accurate. Below is the most likely chronology—according to the current state of research—of the composing of the *Waltzes* and the consequent order in which they appear in our edition:

Waltz in E	WN 18	–	1829
Waltz in B minor	WN 19	–	1829
Waltz in Db	WN 20	– 3 Oct.	1829
Waltz in Ab	WN 28	–	1829–30
Waltz in E minor	WN 29	–	1830 (?)
Waltz in Gb	WN 42	– 8 Aug.	1832
Waltz in Ab	WN 47	– before	1835
Waltz in F minor	WN 55	–	1841
Waltz in A minor	WN 63	–	1847–49

One editorial problem that is particularly pronounced in this volume is the a b u n d a n c e of sources presenting different versions—in most cases undoubtedly authentic—of particular *Waltzes*. This applies to the *Waltzes in B minor*, WN 19 (4 versions), *in Gb*, WN 42 (3 versions), *in Ab*, WN 47 (6 versions), and *in F minor*, WN 55 (6 versions), which were among those most frequently offered by Chopin as keepsakes. Generally written in haste, with more care taken over the aesthetic appearance of the manuscript than the fine-tuning of compositional nuances or the accuracy of the notation, the autographs of these *Waltzes* differ in numerous, often rather insignificant, details. Thus the editors have endeavoured on the one hand to take account of all the significant variants, from details of melody through to overall conception, whilst on the other not overwhelming the pianist with a surfeit of barely audible discrepancies. The choice of the main versions was determined, above all, by the degree to which the particular sources were completed and also —in the case of significant differences in this respect—by the extent of their authenticity and by their chronology. The versions which best meet these criteria are given first (with the letter 'a' by the number).

1. Waltz in E major, WN 18

Sources
[A]   The autograph is not extant.

IJ   Six-bar incipit in the list of 36 *Unpublished Works* by Chopin compiled *c.* 1854 by the composer's sister, Ludwika Jędrzejewicz (Fryderyk Chopin Museum, Warsaw). The text was doubtless taken from [**A**].

[**KC**] Lost copy made by Oskar Kolberg, most probably from [**A**], sent to the Music Society in Lviv as the base text for an edition (see below).

EL   First edition, Lviv 1861. The *Waltz* was included in Lviv Music Society's album of that year. In the heading, by the composer's name, is the note: 'from a manuscript from the year 1829'.

ECh   Second edition, W. Chaberski, Kraków 1871. This reproduces the text of EL with minor additions to performance markings. The reprise, marked in EL as *Da Capo*, is written out in notes, although without bars 1-4. This is certainly an arbitrary revision, as there is nothing to suggest that any other, inextant, sources were used for this edition.

Editorial principles
We give the text of EL.

p. 12   *Bar 4* On the 3rd beat EL has **mf**. We do not give it, as its authenticity is doubtful (Chopin used this sign only exceptionally) and a dynamic marking seems unnecessary here.

2. Waltz in B minor, WN 19

The variety of textual details appearing in the sources for this *Waltz* bids us assume the existence of at least f o u r a u t o g r a p h s, none of which, unfortunately, has survived. However, they can be reconstructed with considerable probability from extant copies and editions, even though their chronology and mutual connections could only be established in part.

Sources
[**AI**] Lost autograph of original version, in 3/8 time, possibly as yet without the *Trio* in B major (see below, **CXI**).

IJ   Four-bar incipit in the list of 36 *Unpublished Works* by Chopin compiled *c.* 1854 by the composer's sister, Ludwika Jędrzejewicz (Fryderyk Chopin Museum, Warsaw). The text was undoubtedly copied—with errors—from [**AI**].

CXI   Copy of original version in 3/8 time, made by an unknown copyist (Kórnik Library, Kórnik-Zamek), probably from [**AI**]. It contains only the main part of the *Waltz* (bars 1-48), which in the initial phase of composition may have constituted the whole work. Apart from three slurs in bars 31-33 **CXI** has no performance markings.

[**A1**] Lost autograph from which **CY** was made (see below). It presents the earlier of the two versions of the whole of the *Waltz*.

CY   Copy made from [**A1**] by an unknown copyist* (Jagiellonian Library, Kraków). The following note by Oskar Kolberg appears at the bottom of the first page: 'The original of the Waltz offered to my brother Wilhelm in 1829 I offer to the Jagiellonian Library, 29 March 1881. O. Kolberg'. In the *Trio* one notes the use of dotted rhythms and the lack of the double notes enriching the second part of the melody (see quotations *about the Waltzes...* before the musical text). It contains numerous performance markings and fingering, possibly Chopin's, mostly written out in pencil.

[**A2**] Lost autograph of the later of the two finished versions of the whole work, possible to reconstruct from an extant copy (**CZ**, see below). In relation to the version of [**A1**] (→**CY**) it displays numerous features of a more mature, generally richer, conception of the work:

---

* The hypothesis encountered in the subject literature that the copyist could have been Wojciech Żywny has yet to be verified, as no sample of his musical script has been found.

— varying of the melodic line of the main part of the *Waltz* (bars 1-48) by means of dotted rhythms (bars 13, 15, 16, 20), grace notes (bars 20, 27-28), a triplet (bar 28) and a turn (bar 44);
— new version of bars 8, 35 and 40-43;
— shifting of the bass line in bars 13-15 and 45-47 down an octave;
— varying of the accompaniment through a more frequent use of rests;
— introduction of B major chord already in bar 48;
— relinquishing of dotted rhythms in the *Trio* (bars 53-78);
— varying of the melody of the *Trio* by means of grace notes (bars 58, 60), mordents (bars 67, 75) and the introduction of the rhythm ♩ ♪ ♪ ♪ (bars 66, 68, 74 and 76);
— use of double notes in the melody of the second part of the *Trio* (bars 64-80).
The version of [**A2**] is distinguished from the remaining sources by having the most meticulously polished accompaniment, with a consistent bass line, and by the well considered arrangement and density of chords.

CZ   Copy of [**A2**] made by an unknown copyist (Bibliothèque Nationale, Paris), notated together with a copy of the *Waltz in Gb*, WN 42, written in the same hand. It contains a number of easily spotted mechanical errors.

[**A3**]   Lost autograph from the album of Countess Plater, from which the first edition was produced by the Kraków publishing firm of Juliusz Wildt (see below). The numerous points of convergence with the version of [**A2**] allow us to see in it an alternative version of the later redaction of the work, yet the premature introduction of certain melodic and harmonic devices shows that Chopin—probably out of haste—failed to ensure the exact placement of particular details, as is indicated by the following:
— change of the bass notes in bars 3 and 11;
— turn as early as bar 12;
— grace notes in bars 19-20, and not bars 27-28;
— two-part writing in the *Trio* already in bar 56.

PE   First Polish edition, I. Wildt, Kraków 1852, also containing the *Waltz in F minor*, WN 55. According to information given on the cover, both *Waltzes* were written into the album of Countess P*** [Plater], in 1844. In **PE** the text of [**A3**] was reproduced (with errors), possibly via the intermediary of a lost copy.

EF   Two almost identical posthumous editions, French and German, edited by Julian Fontana, containing two *Waltzes* (No. 1 *in Ab*, WN 48, No. 2 *in B minor*, WN 19):

FEF   Fontana's French edition, J. Meissonnier Fils (J. M. 3526), Paris July 1855. The text of **FEF** is closest to the version of [**A1**] (→**CY**), yet also contains elements characteristic of the later redaction (new version of bars 40-42, R.H. double notes in the *Trio*), as well as several details which could derive from Chopin, even though they appear in no other source (bars 12-14, 16(1ᵛ)-1, 46). In addition, as in other works which he edited, Fontana certainly made alterations, above all supplementing performance markings (some during printing) and writing out all repeats in full; he is also likely to have interfered in the areas of pitch and rhythm (e.g. changing the thirds a#¹-c#² to the fifths f#¹-c#² in bars 65, 67 & analog. or lowering by an octave the bass note in bar 81). In this situation, it is difficult to state which sources were used to edit **FEF**. Most probably, Fontana based his edition on a manuscript diverging little from **CY**, onto which he superimposed several later versions either taken from another source or only remembered from what he had heard*. This superimposition is most clearly visible in bars 53-56 & analog.: if—as seems likely—the abandoning in **CZ** & **PE** of dotted rhythms in these bars was linked to the introduction of double notes in the second part of the *Trio*, then the combining of these elements in **FEF** may be deemed the effect of an arbitrary compilation of versions.

GEF   Fontana's German edition, A. M. Schlesinger (S. 4395), Berlin July 1855, based on a proof copy of **FEF**. In **GEF** the fascicle containing these two *Waltzes* was given the inauthentic opus number 69. **FEF** & **GEF** differ in respect to some of the performance markings, doubtless as a result of additions made by Fontana during the separate proofreading of each of them.

Editorial principles
We give both the completed versions of the *Waltz*: the later version on the basis of **CZ** and the earlier according to **CY**, both compared with the remaining sources to eliminate mistakes by the copyists. The less polished version of **PE** and the version of **EF**, the extent of the authenticity of which it is difficult to ascertain, are given in the *Appendix* (pp. 46-53).

2a. Later version. We give the text of **CZ**, correcting several unquestionable errors by the copyist. We write out the return of the first part of the *Waltz* (bars 81-96), marked in **CZ** in a simplified manner as a repeat of bars 1-16. In the form of variants we append several alternative versions from **PE** that are most probably Chopin's. We reconstruct the differentiation between long and short accents, marked very imprecisely in **CZ**, taking account of Chopin's habits, familiar from other compositions.
In the further part of this commentary, besides discussing editorial problems relating to the basic source of this version (**CZ**), we also signal all the more important variants of the text of the *Waltz* in the remaining sources. For the sake of identification of the discussed bars, we use the numbering adopted in this version of the *Waltz*; numbering in the remaining versions, particularly **EF**, is different.

p. 14   *Beginning* R.H. The sources contain five different versions of the beginning:

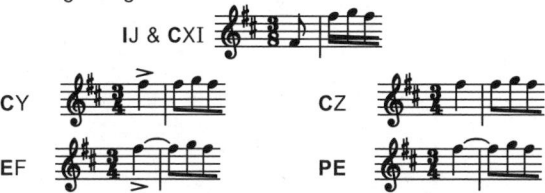

Whilst the lack of a tie or accent could, in some sources, be considered accidental, it seems more likely that Chopin did not have a single fixed way of beginning the *Waltz* (see note to beginning of the *Waltz in F minor*, WN 55). For the main text we adopt the version appearing in the basic source, with the repetition of f#², leaving the possibility of holding this note (with accent or without) as variantal. It is worth noting that in an analogous situation in bars 80-81 **CZ** has both a tie and an accent.

Bar 3 L.H. At the beginning of the bar **PE** has F#, and in the chords additionally a#. The switch of the bass notes in bars 3 & 11 (see note to bar 11) that occurs only in **PE** may possibly be explained as follows: after writing—inadvertently—in bar 3 the version with F#, which was not supposed to appear until bar 11, Chopin decided in the latter bar to write in the version with A# that he had just replaced. This manoeuvre allowed him to retain the differentiation of these bars without making deletions to this souvenir manuscript.

Bars 7, 8 & 40 L.H. In both chords of bar 7 and on the 3ʳᵈ beat of bars 8 and 40 **PE** has additionally c#¹. This may be due to a misreading of the autograph (it can be very difficult in Chopin's autographs to ascertain whether a note placed on a ledger line occurs within a chord; cf., e.g. notes to *Waltz in C# minor*, Op. 64 No. 1, bars 34, 42 & analog. and to *Mazurka in A minor*, WN 60, bars 1, 3, 5...). It is characteristic that wherever four-note chords appear in the sources in the accompaniment of this *Waltz*, one of the notes is always c#¹, which is absent from other sources (some or all). Cf. notes to bar 8 and bars 54 & 72 of version 2b and to bars 3 & 80 of version (2a) in the *Appendix*.

---

* In the afterword to his edition of Chopin's *Oeuvres posthumes*, Fontana wrote: 'not only did I hear the composer play almost all the works in this collection many times, but [...] I also performed them for him, preserving them in my memory ever since just as he created them [...]'.

Bar 8 R.H. As the 6th quaver in the bar the earlier version (**C**XI, **C**Y & **E**F) has $c\#^2$.

Bar 11 L.H. At the beginning of the bar **PE** has *A#*, and in the chords $c\#^1$ instead of *a#*. Cf. note to bar 3.

Bars 11 & 14 R.H. On the 3rd beat of bar 11 and the 1st beat of bar 14 **PE** has the rhythm ♪. ♪, which is most probably an authentic rhythmic variant. As the adopted version of **CZ** has similar rhythms already in the neighbouring bars 13 & 15, the inclusion of the variants from **PE** would result in an excessive concentration of rhythms of this type in the fragment in question. For this reason, we leave the version of **CZ** as the only version. Cf. note to bar 46.

Bar 12 R.H. Above the 3rd beat **PE** has a turn, whilst it is lacking the grace note that ends the bar.

Bars 12-14 & 46 Although not confirmed by other sources, the versions of these bars in **EF** may still be authentic. One notes that bars 14 & 46 are based on an E minor chord with a sixth, which, besides **EF**, appear—in a different form—only in the earliest source, **C**XI.

Bars 13 & 15 R.H. In both bars we give the rhythm on the 1st beat according to **CZ**. All the other sources have even values.

Bars 13-15 L.H. The octaves at the beginning of bars 13-14 appear only in **CZ**. In the other sources the bass is led in the small octave. In bar 15 **CZ** & **PE** have *F#*, the other sources *f#*. Cf. bars 45-47.

Bar 16 L.H. **PE** has the original version (consistent with **C**XI) of the accompaniment.

Bar 16 (1ᵃ volta) – 1 R.H. The progression $c\#^2$-d^2 at the transition between bars that occurs only in **EF** may be authentic.

Bars 17-47 The repeat of these bars (together with the *1ᵃ volta* version of bar 48 that acts as a transition) is marked in **PE** and written out in notes in **EF**. As there are no grounds for questioning its authenticity, we give it in the form of a variant. The transitional bar 48 we give in a footnote in a version with a semiquaver at the end of the bar, congruent with this bar's notation in **PE**, or with a quaver, which appears in **PE** in bar 16.

Bars 17-32 L.H. The earlier sources are characterised by a greater rhythmic uniformity to the accompaniment: the rests on the 3rd beat in **C**XI are entirely absent, in **EF** only bar 31 ends with a rest, and in **C**Y only bars 22, 30 & 31. In **PE**, meanwhile, there are more rests, but this breaks the phrase up into short, two-bar segments.

Bars 19-20 & 27-28 R.H. The grace notes at the beginning of these bars occur in bars 19-20 in **PE** and—more naturally—in bars 27-28 in **CZ**. They are entirely absent from the remaining sources.

Bars 21 & 29 R.H. The main text comes from **CZ**, the variants from **PE**. The remaining sources are convergent with **CZ**.

Bar 24 L.H. On the 3rd beat **CZ** has the chord $f\#$-$c\#^1$-e^1. The convergent version of **C**Y, **PE** & **EF** allows us to deem this a mistake by the copyist.

Bar 25 R.H. The main text comes from **CZ** and the other sources, the variant from **PE**. Grace notes of this type are characteristic of Chopin, cf. e.g. *Nocturnes in F#*, Op. 15 No. 2, bar 52, and *in C minor*, Op. 48 No. 1, bar 19, and the *Concertos, in E minor*, Op. 11, movt. I, bars 607 & 609, and *in F minor*, Op. 21, movt. III, bars 160, 186 & 190.

p. 15

Bar 27 L.H. The chords on the 2nd and 3rd beats are notated in **CZ** with errors: $f\#$-a-g^1 and a-g^1. We give the version of the analogous bar 19, confirmed by **C**Y.

Bar 28 R.H. The triplet on the 3rd beat was introduced in **CZ** & **PE** to vary the melody.

Bar 31 R.H. The rhythm in the main text comes from **CZ** and the remaining sources, that in the variant from **PE**. One notes the convergence between the motivic division marked with slurs in the version of **CZ** with the division marked with a rest in the version of **PE**.

Bars 32-33 L.H. The slur linking *A#* and *B* comes from **C**XI, **C**Y & **EF**.

Bar 34 L.H. At the beginning of the bar **CZ** erroneously has *e*. We give the *c#* appearing in the other sources.

Bars 34 & 36 R.H. **CZ** has here twice the sign *sf*, which Chopin used only exceptionally. We may presume that the copyist involuntarily used this sign—more often employed by other composers—in place of Chopin's *fz*. This supposition is confirmed by the notation of **C**Y, from which we can infer that [**A**2] had here *fz*.

Bar 35 R.H. We give the version of **CZ** & **PE**. In the other sources the 4th and 5th quavers appear in reverse order, $c\#^2$-e^2 (analogously to bar 3).

Bar 38 R.H. In **CZ** the accent appears above the 1st crotchet. As this is most probably an error, we give it—as in the analogous bar 6—above the 3rd crotchet.

Bars 40-43 We give the version of **CZ** & **PE**. In the earlier sources (**C**XI & **C**Y) these bars are a repeat of bars 8-11. **EF** has the later version in bars 40-42 and the earlier version in bar 43.

Bar 43 R.H. The main text of the 3rd beat comes from **CZ**, the variant from **PE**.

Bar 44 R.H. The turn and grace note on the 3rd beat come from **CZ**. In **PE** there is a trill with written-out termination; its execution at a tempo that is natural for the *Waltz* does not differ from the turn. This ornament does not appear in the other sources.

Bars 45-47 L.H. We give the version of **CZ**. The bass in the great octave, albeit in a different pattern, also appears in **PE**.

Bar 46 R.H. The main text of the 1st beat comes from **CZ**. The variant is the version of **PE** that appears solely in the analogous bar 14. We consider such a transferral of versions acceptable since rhythmic variants of this sort, common in Chopin, are not linked closely to the structure of the phrase, but relate purely to performance. A further argument in favour of appending this variant here is the accent on a^2 that appears in the main version, which could also indicate a slight extension of this note.
R.H. As the 3rd and 4th quavers **CZ** erroneously has $b\#^1$-$c\#^2$. As the L.H. part is unquestionably correct, we adopt in the melody the version of the analogous bar 14, confirmed by **C**Y & **PE**.

Bar 48 L.H. $d\#^1$ as the upper note of the sixth on the 2nd beat appears in **CZ** & **PE** alone (remaining sources have d^1). Only in **CZ** is this sixth repeated on the 3rd beat.

Bar 49 The expression *Trio* for the section beginning on the 3rd beat of bar 48 appears only in **C**Y & **PE**.

Bars 49-52 L.H. Only in **CZ** are double notes consistently used on the 2nd and 3rd beats, which, together with the grace notes in the melody in bars 58 & 60, gives a subtle, characteristically Chopinian differentiation of bars 49-52 & 57-60.

Bars 53-56 & analog. R.H. On the 2nd beat in these bars **CZ** & **PE** have even quavers. In equivalent motifs **CY** & **EF** have dotted rhythms.

Bar 56 R.H. As the 2nd quaver on the 2nd beat **CZ** has $d\#^2$. This is certainly an error, as the following testifies:
— the $c\#^2$ that appears in all the other sources;
— the $c\#^2$ that appears in all sources (including **CZ**) in the analogous bar 72.

Bars 56-64 In **PE** the melody is two-part from the 3rd beat of bar 56. In the editors' opinion, the introduction of this effect as early as the second of the four eight-bar units of the *Trio* resulted from Chopin's inattention and haste in writing out [A3]. In the version of **CZ** adopted by us, the two-part writing appears in a natural way half-way through the *Trio*, as a further enrichment—following the grace notes in bars 58 and 60—of the basic phrase of this section.

Bar 60 L.H. In the chords on the 2nd and 3rd beats **CZ** does not have $c\#^1$. This is most probably a misreading of [A2] by the copyist (cf. note to bars 7, 8 & 40).

Bar 61 L.H. The main text comes from **CZ**, the variant from **EF**. This same harmonic change, albeit written with the use of dyads— $f\#$-$d\#^1$ followed by $g\#$-$d\#^1$—also appears in **PE**. It is difficult to say whether in **CZ** Chopin purposely left the original version, or whether he simply forgot about this slight varying of the harmony. Also possible is an error on the part of the copyist, who may have overlooked the change to the chord. A similar harmonic alternative in a similar context occurs in the *Waltz in A♭*, WN 28, bars 11-12.

Bar 62 L.H. As the top note of both chords **CZ** erroneously has $a\#^1$.

p. 16 *Bars 65, 67 & analog.* R.H. As the 4th quaver **EF** has in these bars the fifth $f\#^1$-$c\#^2$. The authenticity of this version seems very doubtful given the convergent, more natural version of **CZ** & **PE**.

Bars 66, 68 & analog. R.H. The rhythm │♩ ♪♩│ appears only in **CZ**.

Bars 67 & 75 R.H. The mordents appear only in **CZ**.

Bar 68 R.H. At the beginning of the bar **CZ** erroneously has the ninth $f\#^1$-$g\#^2$.

Bar 69 L.H. As the top note of the chord on the 2nd beat **CZ** has, most probably erroneously, $f\#^1$.

Bar 70 R.H. In **EF** the lower note of the dyads on the 2nd and 3rd beats is $c\#^2$.

Bar 72 R.H. On the 3rd beat **PE** has the octave $f\#^1$-$f\#^2$.

Bar 73 In **PE** & **EF** the key of B minor appears already in this bar. We leave as the only version that of **CZ**—confirmed by **CY** —in which this bar is still based on a B major chord. In this version, the transition from B major to B minor occurs in a gradual way, as is characteristic of Chopin: first (bar 74) there appears the lowered VI degree g^2, and only then (bar 75) the third of the minor tonic, d^2. Cf. e.g. *Mazurka in B minor*, Op. 33 No. 4, bars 161-164, *Etude in B minor*, Op. 25 No. 10, bars 90-95.

Bar 76 R.H. In **CZ** the bar ends with triads:

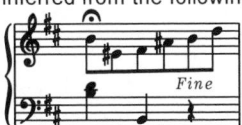 (the lack of the quaver flag on the 1st of these chords is obviously an error). In the editors' opinion, the notes e^2 were written here by mistake:
— e^2 does not have a direct resolution in the following bar;
— $a\#^1$ as the lower note of the dyad in the close of the bar is confirmed by the version in both **PE** and **EF**;
— there are no triads in the R.H. anywhere in this *Waltz* (in any of the sources).

Bars 77-80 The close of the *Trio* has a distinctly different form in each of the sources:

We give the version of **CZ**, which raises no particularly serious doubts. In the **EF** version there is some doubt as to the authenticity of the combining of the original version of the melody (containing semiquavers and convergent with **CY**) with its two-part arrangement. In the version of **PE** a possible error is the F# instead of B at the beginning of bar 77.

Bar 80 L.H. As the top note of the chord **CZ** has $a\#^1$. This is most probably an error by the copyist:
— $a\#^1$ is held in the R.H.;
— the simplicity of the *Waltz*'s texture makes the use in the accompaniment of a note higher than the melodic note ($f\#^1$ on the 2nd beat) very unlikely;
— the copyist made an identical error in bar 62, and similar errors also in bars 27, 68 & 69.

Bars 81-96 In **CZ** these bars are marked as a repeat of bars 1-16 (*Dal segno al fine*), where the appearance of bar 96 is to be inferred from the following notation of bar 16:

2b. Earlier version. We give the text of **CY**, correcting obvious errors. Bars 38-48, marked in **CY** as a repeat (*Dal Segno*) of bars 6-16, we write out in notes. We include the fingering that may come from Chopin.

F o r m . It is not clear whether the return of the main section (B minor) following the *Trio* is to encompass the whole section (bars 1-48) or the first period (bars 1-16) only. This is due to the fact that in **CY** the main section itself is already written with the use of an abbreviation—it ends in bar 37 with the instruction *Dal Segno al fine e poi*, which means returning to bar 6 (*Segno*), continuing thence to bar 16 (*Fine*) and then moving on to the *Trio*. This placement of *Fine* renders the instruction *Valce* (sic) *da capo al fine*, appearing after the *Trio*, ambiguous, as it can be understood in two different ways:
— 'waltz from the beginning to the (closest) instruction *Fine*', and so the repetition of bars 1-16 only;
— 'waltz from the beginning to the end'—the repetition of bars 1-48.
The other sources tend to indicate the former interpretation—in **CZ** the *Waltz* unquestionably ends with the repetition of bars 1-16, in **PE** it is not marked how the work should end, and **EF**, which has a complete, 48-bar, reprise, is not reliable in this respect (Fontana usually sought to expand the works he was editing as much as possible). Hence our marking of the end of the *Waltz* in bar 16.

p. 17   *Bar 8* L.H. The notes $c\#^1$ could have found their way into the chords in **CY** as a result of the copyist's misreading of the autograph. **CXI** has here triads, without $c\#^1$. Cf. note to version 2a, bars 7, 8 & 40.

p. 18   *Bar 36* R.H. The lack of the $f\!\!\!x$ is certainly an oversight by the copyist, who started to write here already the *Dal Segno* from the next bar.

p. 19   *Bars 54 & 72* L.H. **CY** has four-note chords in these bars. Comparison with the analogous bars 70 & 56 leads to the conclusion that the notes $c\#^2$ could have been written here by mistake. Cf. note to bars 7, 8 & 40 of version 2a.

Bar 60 R.H. As the last note of the bar **CY** erroneously has e^2.

Bar 77 L.H. In **CY** the ♮ lowering $d\#^1$ to d^1 is missing in front of the top note of the chord on the 2nd beat.

Bar 78 R.H. In front of the 1st note of the bar **CY** has ♯ instead of ♮. This is certainly an error, as the gradual preparation for the B minor key beginning with the entry of g^2 in bar 75, precludes such a use of $d\#^2$ here.
L.H. In **CY** there is no sign in front of the 1st note in the bar, which gives G♯. This possibly original version we give in the main text. In the variant with G, meanwhile, we take account of the entirely likely omission of ♮:
— G appears in all the other sources;
— the mistake in the R.H. in this bar and the lack of the ♮ in the previous bar point to a probable lapse in the writer's concentration towards the end of the work.

3. Waltz in D flat major, WN 20

Sources
[AW] Lost autograph, sent on 3 Oct. 1829 to Tytus Woyciechowski (see quotations *about the Waltzes...* before the musical text).
[AE] Lost autograph from the album of Emilia Elsner. Its existence is mentioned several times by Ferdynand Hoesick*.
IJ   Four-bar incipit in Ludwika Jędrzejewicz's list of *Unpublished Works* (see note to *Waltz in E*, WN 18). We may assume that this was copied from the same manuscript from which Julian Fontana prepared his edition.
EF   Two almost identical posthumous editions, French and German, edited by Julian Fontana, containing three *Waltzes* (No. 1 *in Gb*, WN 42, No. 2 *in F minor*, WN 55, No. 3 *in Db*, WN 20):
FEF   Fontana's French edition, J. Meissonnier Fils (J. M. 3527), Paris July 1855. Given the lack of extant manuscripts, it is difficult to say on which of them—[AW] or [AE], or possibly another—Fontana based his text. This edition bears traces of revisions that are typical of Fontana's editing: the writing-out of repeats, which in the autograph were doubtless marked with repeat signs, and the supplementing of performance markings.
GEF   Fontana's German edition, A. M. Schlesinger (S. 4396), Berlin July 1855, doubtless based on a proof of **FE**F. In **GE**F the fascicle containing these three *Waltzes* was given the inauthentic opus number 70.

Editorial principles
We give the text of **FE**F, correcting the most probable errors or revisions by Fontana. We remove performance markings which are very unlikely to be authentic (metronome tempos, initial tempo, *mf* and others). We mark with repeat signs the repeats of bars 1-8 & 9-16.

---

* F. Hoesick, 'Józef Elsner i pierwsze Konserwatorium w Warszawie. (Z papierów i pamiątek po Elsnerze)' [Józef Elsner and the first Conservatory in Warsaw. (From Elsner's papers and mementoes], *Biblioteka Warszawska*, VII 1900.

p. 20   *Beginning* **EF** gives here *Moderato* ♩=108. These markings were certainly added by Fontana, as in waltzes not intended for print Chopin rarely specified tempo verbally (it was unnecessary for a dance that was so fashionable at that time), and he gave a metronome tempo in none of his waltzes.

Bar 1 R.H. In some later collective editions the two notes f^2 were arbitrarily tied.

Bar 8 (2ª volta) R.H. As the last quaver **EF** has c^2 (version given in the footnote). One may doubt whether this note corresponds to Chopin's intentions, as he usually ends melodic phrases of this sort with a note of the chord that forms the harmonic background of the given bar or with a passing note that connects such a note melodically with the next (often one and the other). Cf. e.g. *Waltzes in B minor*, WN 19, bar 16, *in Eb*, Op. 18, bar 172, *in C♯ minor*, Op. 64 No. 2, bars 39-40 & analog., *Concerto in F minor*, Op. 21, movt. III, bars 425 & 427. Here, the c^2 in question is a foreign note: it neither belongs to the Db major chord nor leads to either of the melodic notes in the following bar (f^2 and its resolution eb^2).
The version with db^2 proposed by the editors is satisfactory in melodic, harmonic and pianistic terms, cf. similar devices e.g. in the *Waltz in A minor*, Op. 34 No. 2, bars 37-38 & analog.

Bar 9 **EF** has here *mf*. We remove it, as Chopin used this marking only exceptionally and its authenticity here is highly dubious.

Bar 17 The term *Trio* does not appear in **EF**, yet Chopin used it to identify this section in a letter to a friend (see quotations *about the Waltzes...* before the musical text).

Bars 17 & 41 L.H. From a description of the phrase that begins in these bars (see quotations *about the Waltzes...* before the musical text), we learn that Chopin was anxious to emphasise the L.H. melody, yet this is not reflected in the performance markings contained in **EF**. For this reason we add the expression *ben marcato il canto*, taking a lead from the *Polonaise in Bb*, WN 17 (bar 82), written around the same time.

Bars 21-23 & 45-47 L.H. We supplement the slurs and set them in order, based on the analogous bars 29-30 & 53-54. **EF** has here only a slur over the quavers in bars 21 & 45.

p. 21   *Bar 32 (2ª volta)* R.H. At the end of the bar **EF** has the triad db^1-gb^1-bb^1. The burdening of the anacrusis with a triad is surely an error, as in this type of context with a rest in the L.H. Chopin most commonly employed single notes, and not once did he use a triad in a *Waltz*. For this reason, we leave only the melodic note bb^1.

Bar 56 **FE**F has here the expression *Fine o da Capo*. This was certainly added by Fontana, who—probably due to unclear markings in the manuscript at his disposal—was uncertain whether Chopin wished for a return of the first section of the *Waltz*. The term *Trio*, used by Chopin in respect to the Gb major section (cf. quotations *about the Waltzes...* before the musical text), confirms unequivocally his intention to impart to this *Waltz* a *da Capo* form, more natural for this dance.

4. Waltz in A flat major, WN 28

This *Waltz* is the only Chopin waltz preserved intact that is written in 3/8 time. There were doubtless at least two autographs of this *Waltz* in existence. An assessment of their mutual relationship is hindered by the fact that the text of one of them is known to us only indirectly, and the edition based on it contains a number of places in which the text of the autograph is believed to have been deformed. We can state, however, that the work was completed in the two autographs to a similar extent.

There are also no grounds on which to order the two autographs chronologically.

Sources

ALB Autograph from the album of Paulina Le Brun, with Chopin's signature, no date (Warsaw Music Society).

[AE] Lost autograph from the album of Emilia Elsner (see commentary to *Waltz in Db*, WN 20), from which the first edition was produced.

E First edition, Breitkopf & Härtel (Klav. Bibl. 23183 II), Leipzig 1902, based on [AE], doubtless via a lost copy. A number of places in the text of E give rise to the suspicion that either the copyist or the engraver misread [AE]; the most important of these are as follows:
— the writing-out in notes of the repeat of bars 1-16 and the marking of this whole 32-bar fragment to be repeated;
— the quaver c^3 instead of the rest on the 2nd R.H. beat in bar 16 (2^a *volta*);
— the last semiquaver of the R.H. (db^2) in bar 24 (2^a *volta*);
— the accompaniment of the *Trio* in bars 41, 42 & 45.
E also contains several alternative versions in relation to ALB that are unquestionably Chopin's.

Editorial principles

We give the certain text of the extant autograph ALB, writing out in notes bars 25-40, marked in ALB in short (*Dal Segno*). As variants we cite those versions of E which raise no doubts with regard to their authenticity.

p. 22 *Bars 1-16* In E the repeat of these bars is written out in notes and ends with a repeat sign after the 2nd quaver of bar 32 of this edition (2^a *volta* bar 16 according to the numbering adopted in our edition). Given the structure of the melody (a quite large amount of repeated motifs) and the uniformity of the rhythm, the expansion of this section to 64 performed bars is certainly an extraneous addition, possibly resulting from a misunderstanding of abbreviations in the manuscript.

Bar 5 & analog. L.H. We give the chords on the 2nd and 3rd quavers as notated in ALB. In bar 5 E has g-bb-db^1 twice, and in analogous bars eb-bb-db^1; the latter chords presumably correspond to the notation of [AE].

Bar 7 & analog. R.H. In ALB the ♭ restoring ab^1 is missing in front of the last semiquaver. Omissions of this type are the most common errors made by Chopin. E has the ♭ in bar 7, but not in its repetitions, which allows us to surmise that this sign was also absent from [AE].

Bars 11-12 L.H. The main text comes from ALB, the variant from E. Similar progressions occur on a number of occasions in Chopin's *Waltzes*: cf. e.g. *Waltzes in B minor*, WN 19, bar 61, *in Ab*, WN 48, bar 8, *in C# minor*, Op. 64 No. 2, bars 66-67 & 70-71.

Bar 16 (2^a volta) The word *Fine* here appears in ALB, but relates to the expression *Dal Segno al fine*, with which Chopin marked bars 25-40 as a repeat of bars 1-16. It is not entirely certain whether, when executing the *Da Capo* after the *Trio*, the work should be ended in bar 16 or bar 40. For reasons discussed in more detail in the commentary to the *Waltz in B minor*, WN 19 (see above, remark on the form of the earlier version of that *Waltz*), we adopt the first of these possibilities. In E *Fine* appears in the last bar of the main section of the *Waltz*.

Bar 16 (2^a volta) & 40 R.H. On the 2nd beat E has a quaver c^3 instead of a rest:  . The authenticity of this version is highly dubious—in phrase endings of this type Chopin usually commences the subsequent idea after a rest, which gives a brief pause in the melody and also allows for the hand to be comfortably shifted, cf. e.g. *Waltzes in E*, WN 18, bars 56 & 72, *in Db*,

WN 20, bars 16 (2^v), 32 & 40, *in E minor*, WN 29, bars 24, 88 & analog., *in Ab*, Op. 34 No. 1, bars 40, 64 & analog., *in F*, Op. 34 No. 3, bar 32 & analog., *in C# minor*, Op. 64 No. 2, bar 48 & analog.

Bars 17-24 The main text (8 bars with repeat) is the version of ALB, whilst the 16-bar variant given at the bottom of the page comes from E. The musical merits of each of these versions are quite clear:
— (ALB) the differentiated character of the f o u r - b a r phrases, resulting from the differing accompaniment pattern, emphasised by the slurring in the R.H. and the accent in bar 19;
— (E) a similar differentiation of the character of e i g h t - b a r segments, with a subtly enhanced ending to the first eight-bar unit (in bar 23 a crotchet in the L.H. instead of a quaver with rest) and beginning to the second (quaver c^3 in the following bar, analogous to the c^3 at the end of bar 16).

Bar 18 L.H. In ALB the note c^1 is missing from the 2nd chord, certainly by accident: this note appears consistently in the other chords of this segment. Chopin either forgot to write it in or else wrote it so unclearly that it merged into the ledger line. E has here a four-note chord with c^1.

p. 23 *Bar 24 (2^a volta)* L.H. On the 2nd beat ALB has a chord with c^1, and we give this uncontroversial version in the main text. It is not entirely certain, meanwhile, whether the sixth ab-f^1 appearing here in E was actually written in [AE], or whether the lack of c^1 should be ascribed to an inexact reading of the manuscript. Since the version with the sixth may be authentic, we include it in the alternative version of bars 17-24 given at the bottom of the page.
R.H. As the last note E has db^2. However, the ♭ placed before it was doubtless printed by mistake instead of ♮, as no chromatic sign would have been necessary to notate db^2. For this reason, we give the version of ALB alone.

Bars 41-42 & 45-46 L.H. In E the accompaniment has the following form:

The authenticity of this version is most probably questionable, as is suggested by inconsistencies among analogous two-bar segments (cf. the wholly regular version of ALB), which needlessly complicate this very simple music. In the editors' opinion the following reconstruction of the version of [AE] is the most likely:

However, as this is merely supposition, we give the version of ALB alone.

5. Waltz in E minor, WN 29

No authentic sources of this *Waltz* have survived, nor any information which unquestionably relates to the circumstances of its composing. Oskar Kolberg associated it with a letter written by Chopin to Tytus Woyciechowski (see quotations *about the Waltzes...* before the musical text); this assumption, expressed in a letter written by Kolberg to Woyciechowski, was not directly confirmed due to the death of the addressee. However, it does seem likely:
— we know of no other *Waltz* to which Chopin could have been referring in this letter;

— the *Polonaise in Gb*, WN 35, also presented in 1830 to Tytus Woyciechowski, was published by the firm of J. Kaufmann, the first publisher of the *Waltz*;
— the work's stylistic features do not preclude the possibility that it was written during the period immediately preceding the date of Chopin's letter (1830).

Sources

[A] The autograph is not extant.
PE1 First Polish edition, Joseph Kaufmann (J 159 K), Warsaw 1868, presumably based on **[A]**, most probably via a purpose-made copy. The text of **PE1** bears traces of revision by the publisher (supplementing of performance markings, writing-out of repeats), and is not free of errors.
PE2 Second impression of **PE1** (same firm and number), in which several flaws are amended and work has begun on revising the chords in bar 90 & analog.
PE3 Third impression of **PE1** (same firm and number), in which the revision of the chords in bar 90 & analog. has been completed and several further changes have been made.
PE4 Fourth impression of **PE1** (same firm and number), in which minor additions have been made to the articulation markings.
PE = **PE1**, **PE2**, **PE3** & **PE4**.
GE First German edition, Les Fils de B. Schott (19551), Mainz 1868, based on **PE1** (the copy of **PE1** on which this edition is based, containing the additions made by the reviser of **GE**, is extant).

Editorial principles

We give the text of **PE1**, correcting certain and probable errors. We reduce the number of pedal signs, bringing them in line with the density of markings encountered in authentic sources of other *Waltzes* not prepared by Chopin for print. We introduce—most probably in line with the notation of **[A]**—repeat signs for the repetition of bars 89-112, written out in notes in the sources (we give this repeat the bar-numbers in square brackets [89-112]).

p. 24 *Bars 1-8* R.H. The sources have separate slurs for bars 1-3, 4 and 5-8. The breaks in the slurring here are presumed to be purely graphically motivated (change in the direction of the beams or move to a new line in the manuscript). Cf. note to bars 139-142.

Bar 12 R.H. On the 3rd beat the sources have a rest. Comparison with all the later appearances of this theme (bars 20, 44, 52 & 116) leads to the conclusion that this is most probably an error, caused either by a misreading of this place (the rest and b^1 lie at the same height) or by the mistaken writing here of the rests from bar 8.

Bar 36 R.H. Above the 1st beat the sources give the fingering digit 4 (as in bars 34 & 38). This seems to be an error, as in such instances Chopin usually placed the 4th finger on the black key and the 5th on the white (cf. e.g. Chopin's fingering in the *Etudes in A minor*, Op. 25 No. 11, bar 82, and *in F*, Op. 10 No. 8, bars 89-90, and in the *Concerto in F minor*, Op. 21, movt. III, bars 97 & 101-102).

p. 25 *Bars 71 & 111* R.H. In **PE1** (→**PE2**, **GE**) the beginning of the bar is notated in the following way: [music example]. In **PE3** this was

changed to a notation analogous to that of bar 87: [music example].

In the editors' opinion, neither of these—essentially equivalent—notations corresponds to the execution intended by Chopin. The reading of grace notes adopted in our edition makes understandable the differentiation of their form (♪ & ♫). The execution of this figure corresponds to the notation used by Chopin e.g. in the *Waltz in Ab*, Op. 34 No. 1, bars 28-29, and beginning the bar with a broken sixth matches the motifs in the preceding bars.

p. 26 *Bars 90 & 92* R.H. The impressions of **PE** differ in the sound of the first chord:

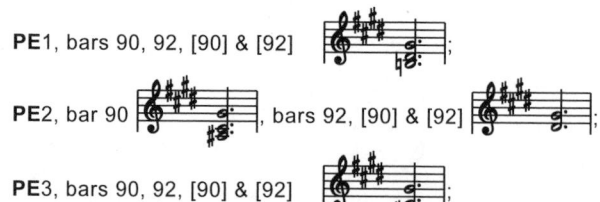

PE1, bars 90, 92, [90] & [92]

PE2, bar 90 ... , bars 92, [90] & [92]

PE3, bars 90, 92, [90] & [92]

All of these versions are doubtless inauthentic:
— the first probably results from a misreading or revision of the manuscript, e.g. through the addition of a ♮ in place of a possibly lacking ♯; Chopin generally juxtaposed chords in parallel keys as an element of modulation and there is never any uncertainty as to the key, as occurs here;
— the second and third are successive phases of a later revision (for reasons unknown, in three of the four places in **PE2** the changes were not completed); there is nothing to suggest that this could have reflected some authentic version of the text.
We give what we consider the most probable reconstruction of **[A]**, based on **PE1**. **GE** also has this version.

Bars 105-106 In **PE** the pedal markings are incomplete: there is only the sign ✳ at the end of bar 106. In the written-out repeat of this fragment—bars [105-106]—there is one pedal per bar. It is difficult from this to determine whether Chopin intended in this two-bar fragment one pedal or two.

Bar 111 L.H. As the 2nd quaver **PE1** & **PE2** have d#. In **PE3** (→**PE4**) and **GE** the error was corrected.

p. 27 *Bar 115* At the beginning of the bar the sources have *p*. The repetition of the sign from bar 113 is doubtless an error here.

Bar 116 L.H. As the 1st note **PE** has the unquestionably erroneous B_1 instead of *g*, which appears in all analogous bars. This is due to mistakes in the notation of changes in clef, as becomes clear when we look at the whole line of text (bars 113-118):

Bar 124 The arpeggio before the 1st chord in the L.H. appears only in **PE1** (→**GE**); in subsequent impressions, it was mistakenly removed during corrections to the graphically awkward placement of the clef (in **PE** this bar begins a new system).
The *staccato* wedges and *sf* were added during the proofreading of **PE2**, probably in line with the base text. We give the latter marking as *fz*, which Chopin used much more often.

Bar 133 R.H. In some later collective editions the first of the group of four quavers was arbitrarily altered to a^2.

Bars 139-142 R.H. In each of these bars the group of quavers is embraced in the sources by a separate slur. In uniform progressions of this sort consecutive slurs denoted simply a *legato* articulation. As they have no bearing on the construction of motifs or phrases, we replace them with a single slur, in line with the modern-day understanding of these signs. Cf. note to bars 1-8.

6. Waltz in G flat major, WN 42

The basic sources from which we are currently familiar with this *Waltz* are two autographs* and the first (posthumous) edition, produced by Julian Fontana. In Fontana's edition, one notes a clearer contrast between the two sections of the work than in the autographs, achieved

---

* Both autographs were found and published in facsimile form with transcription by Byron Janis: Chopin/Janis, *The Most Dramatic Musical Discovery of the Age*, Envolve Books, USA 1978.

above all through a simpler, uniform rhythm to the melody in each of the sections (the lack of semiquavers in the main section and the lack of semiquaver rests in the middle section). It seems impossible that Fontana could have made such far-reaching changes arbitrarily, which leads to the conclusion that his edition must have been based on a third, now lost, autograph, presenting a different conception of the work. Moreover, thanks to the known dates for the writing of the two extant autographs (1832 & 1833), it is possible to state that the direction of the changes displayed by the rhythm and character of the second autograph in relation to the first leads consistently to the third version documented in Fontana's edition:

— in the melody of bars 1-24 the rhythms ♩.♪ & ♪♫ appear—counting all repetitions—42 times in the 1832 autograph, only 21 times in the 1833 text and not once in Fontana's edition; by way of example, here are the versions of the first 4 bars in this order of the sources:

—in bars 25-48 Chopin gradually relinquishes ♪♫ rhythms in favour of ♪.♪. In the 1832 autograph the rhythm ♩.♩ appears only in bars 32(2ᵛ)-35. In the later text the proportions are reversed: it is the rhythm ♪♫ that appears only in bar 25 & analog., completely disappearing in the edition. Here are the source versions of the opening four-bar segment of this section:

This allows us to infer that the third, lost, autograph was produced later than the two extant texts. This hypothesis is confirmed by the date—1835—ascribed to the *Waltz* by Fontana in his edition, which is presumably the year the third autograph was produced. It also seems worth emphasising that the latest version is—due to the calmer rhythm of the R.H. leaps and the change of bb^1 to db^2 in bar 4 & analog.—the most comfortable to play.

Sources

A1 Autograph (1 page) dated 'Paris, 8/8 [18]32' (Yale University, New Haven). The earliest of the known copies of the *Waltz*, it is characterised by the greatest number of dotted rhythms in the main section (bars 1-16 of the autograph).

CZ Copy by an unknown copyist (Bibliothèque Nationale, Paris), notated together with a copy, in the same hand, of the *Waltz in B minor*, WN 19. It was made from **A**1 or—more probably—its other, lost copy. It contains decidedly fewer performance markings than **A**1 and a number of mechanical, easily spotted, errors. In bar 25 one notes the grace note db^2, which is absent from **A**1.

A2 Autograph (2 pages) undated (Château Thoiry), which information recorded by its first owner dates at 1833. Despite numerous differences from the version of **A**1, the *Waltz* retains the same overall character.

[A3**]** Lost autograph of a different, most mature, conception of the *Waltz*, possible to reconstruct thanks to Fontana's edition, based on this text.

EF Two almost identical posthumous editions, French and German, edited by Julian Fontana, containing three *Waltzes* (No. 1 *in Gb*, WN 42, No. 2 *in F minor*, WN 55, No. 3 *in Db*, WN 20):

FEF Fontana's French edition, J. Meissonnier Fils (J. M. 3527), Paris July 1855, based—doubtless via a purposely-made copy—on [**A**3]. This edition bears traces of revisions that are characteristic of Fontana's editing (all repeats written out in notes, performance markings supplemented and probably also other arbitrary changes).

GEF Fontana's German edition, A. M. Schlesinger (S. 4396), Berlin July 1855, doubtless based on a proof of **FEF**. In **GEF** the fascicle with the three *Waltzes* was given the inauthentic opus number 70.

Editorial principles

Each of the three autographs presents a different redaction of the *Waltz*—all three elaborated in detail. The versions of the extant autographs are closer to each other than to what is most probably the latest redaction [**A**3]. In this situation, we give all three versions, giving priority to the latest.

6a. Version of the latest autograph. We give the text of **EF**, eliminating elements of dubious authenticity, such as metronomic tempo markings and supplementary pedalling. In keeping with Chopin's customary practice, we mark the repeats of bars 17-24, 25-32 & 33-48 by means of repeat signs, and the return of bars 1-16 as *Da Capo*. In places where, due to errors or to Fontana's revisions, one may suspect a deformation of Chopin's intentions, we give alternative versions from **A**1 or **A**2 which are unquestionably Chopin's. We supplement or correct obvious minor inaccuracies of slurring, according to analogous passages. Fingering with the features of authenticity is given without brackets.

In the further part of the commentary, besides the discussion of editorial problems relating to the basic source of this version (**EF**), we signal all the more important variants of the text of the *Waltz* in the other sources.

p. 28 *Beginning & bar 25* At the beginning of the work **EF** gives **Molto vivace**, and in bar 24 *molto ritenuto*. In both expressions we omit the word 'molto', possibly added by Fontana, who had a tendency to magnify contrasts (in the *Waltzes* prepared by Chopin for print **Vivace** is the most frequently used tempo marking).
For the two parts of the *Waltz* **EF** gives the metronome tempo – ♩. = 88 at the beginning and ♩ = 96 in bar 25; these were certainly added by Fontana, as Chopin indicated a metronome tempo in none of his *Waltzes*.

Bars 4 & 12 R.H. As the 5ᵗʰ (lowest) note of the melody **A**1 (→**CZ**) & **A**2 have bb^1 (against a correspondingly lower accompaniment). In addition, these manuscripts have at the end of each of these bars an additional semiquaver c^2, not appearing in the version of **EF**.

Bars 6 & 14 R.H. In **A**1 (→**CZ**) & **A**2 the motifs in these bars have an identical structure as in bars 7 & 15 (an extra gb^2 at the end of the bar).

Bars 9 & 17 In the repeats of these bars written out in notes **EF** has ***p*** signs. Adding markings that created dynamic contrasts was one of Fontana's favourite editorial devices, hence our omission of these doubtless inauthentic signs.

Bar 16 In **A**2 the anacrusis to the Db major section has a distinctly different form: the melodic motif, shortened to its last two notes, is accompanied by an Eb minor chord struck on the 3ʳᵈ beat.

Bars 16 & 48 (2ᵃ volta) L.H. In **EF** the last note has the value of a crotchet, as the return of bars 1-16 after the middle section is written out entirely in notes. We adopt the notation of **A**1 (→**CZ**).

Bars 19 & 23 R.H. In the double grace note **A**1 (→**CZ**) & **A**2 have gb^3 as the second note instead of the f^3 in **EF**.

Bar 24 (1ª volta) R.H. In **A**1 (→**CZ**) & **A**2 the melody of both versions (1ª & 2ª volta) of this bar is identical. The motif referring back to the beginning of the *Waltz* which appears in **EF** seems a favourable differentiation.

p. 29 *Bars 25 & 41* R.H. As the grace note **EF** has in both bars the third bb^1-db^2. In neither case is the third adequately explained by either the sound or the voice-leading; hence we give the grace notes in the version transmitted by the manuscripts: the db^2 in bar 25 appears in **CZ**, the bb^1 in bar 41 in **A**1 (→**CZ**) & **A**2.

Bars 28 & 44 L.H. The triads on the 2nd and 3rd crotchets appear in **EF**, the open fifths in **A**1 (→**CZ**) & **A**2. We admit both possibilities, as the inconsistent sound of the version of **EF**—a transparent dominant chord (without the fifth) in bars 27 & 43, resolving on a doubled tonic triad in the bars under discussion—raises doubts with regard to style.

Bar 32 (1ª volta) R.H. The version of **EF** (our variant) may cause doubts with regard to style: the 'burdening' of the end of the eight-bar unit with thirds and a change to the melody that weakens the link with the preceding bars (motif of three repeated notes, characteristic of the whole section). Since a stylistic awkwardness, suggesting editorial interference, appears several times in such endings to a regular eight-bar structure in works edited by Fontana (cf. notes to *Funeral March in C minor*, WN 9, bar 26, *Ecossaises in G*, WN 13 No. 1, bar 4(2ᵛ), and *in D*, WN 13 No. 3, bar 8(1ᵛ), and *Mazurka in G*, WN 26, bar 20(1ᵛ)), we give as the main version the essentially convergent text of **A**1 (→**CZ**) & **A**2 (the manuscripts differ solely in the form of the rhythm on the 3rd beat).

Bars 33-36 L.H. As the main text we give the version of the extant autographs, on the basis of **A**1 (→**CZ**) (**A**2 has octaves at the beginning of bars 33-34 – see version 6b). The version of **EF** differs from this in several crucial details: d^1 instead of f^1 in the chords of bar 33, octaves instead of chords on the 2nd and 3rd beats of bar 34, and a lowered bass in bar 36 (cf. note to *Waltz in F minor*, WN 55, bars 6-8). Without access to the lost [**A**3], it is difficult to say whether these differences were introduced by Chopin or result from errors or alterations made by Fontana. For this reason, we give the less certain version of **EF** in the variants.

Bar 36 L.H. Beneath the 2nd and 3rd crotchets **EF** has a ‿ sign instead of a slur. As this is most probably a misreading of [**A**3], we replace it with the slur appearing in **A**2.

Bar 38 R.H. In the manuscripts the bar ends with an A♭ minor chord. The earlier introduction in **EF** of the A♭ major chord, which with an added seventh appears in the next bar, is a characteristically Chopinian harmonic device (cf. e.g. *Ballade in G minor*, Op. 23, bar 21).

6b. Version of the earlier autograph. We give the text of **A**2.

p. 31 *Bar 45* R.H. The main text is a literal reading of the version of **A**2. The variant is a version modelled on the three analogous bars 25, 29 & 41. The distances between successive thirds in **A**2 suggest that Chopin, in writing the note-heads, intended to repeat the rhythm of this phrase in an unaltered form. Today it is impossible to determine whether the even quavers that were ultimately written attest that Chopin failed to complete the notation or constitute a conscious varying of rhythm.

6c. Version of the earliest autograph. We give the text of **A**1. As a variant version we include the grace note appearing in bar 25 in **CZ**.

p. 33 *Bar 25* R.H. The grace note db^2 comes from **CZ**, where it was written in twice: at the beginning of bar 25 and at the end of bar 32 (1ª volta). The latter entry appears to testify some misunderstanding. The authenticity of the grace note in bar 25 is supported by the lack in **CZ** of any traces of extraneous additions, be it in this *Waltz* or in the *Waltz in B minor*, WN 19.

7. Waltz in A flat major, WN 47

The composing of this *Waltz* is generally associated with Chopin's week-long stay with the Wodziński family in Dresden in September 1835 (see quotations *about the Waltzes...* before the musical text), during which he wrote the *Waltz* into the album of the 16-year-old Maria Wodzińska. However, extant copies of the original version of the work prove that it must have been written earlier, and perhaps only further polished in Dresden. In later years Chopin offered autographs of this *Waltz* to several other individuals.

Sources

[**AI**] Lost (working?) autograph of the original version, with simpler texture and harmony. Many rhythmic details were also changed in the later sources. The reconstruction of [**AI**] is possible thanks to extant copies (see below, **C**XI, Fr**C**I & Fr**C**II).

CXI Copy of the original version (Bibliothèque Nationale, Paris), made by an unknown copyist, probably from [**AI**], retaining the original way of notating bars 33-48 as a repeat *dal segno* of bars 1-16.

Fr**C**I Copy by Auguste Franchomme with dedication for Jane W. Stirling, 22 May 1850 (Biblioteka Jagiellońska, Kraków). The date on the manuscript is not connected with the copied autograph and is doubtless the date the copy was made or offered. Fr**C**I presents a version of the *Waltz* that is very similar to the version of **C**XI, and assuming that Chopin made minor adjustments in [**AI**] after **C**XI was prepared, it may have been copied from this autograph. Franchomme wrote out bars 33-48 in notes, doubtless wishing to facilitate the reading of the manuscript.

Fr**C**II Copy by Franchomme dedicated to his daughter Cécile, May 1850 (Bibliothèque Nationale, Paris). This was initially, like Fr**C**I, a copy of the original version, but Franchomme subsequently modified it through erasure and deletion to the version of **A**3. The original text, legible in many places, allows us to identify several errors in Fr**C**I.

Fr**C** = Fr**C**I & original notation of Fr**C**II (wherever this is legible).

IJ Four-bar incipit in the list of 36 *Unpublished Works* by Chopin compiled *c.* 1854 by the composer's sister, Ludwika Jędrzejewicz (Fryderyk Chopin Museum, Warsaw). Marked with the note, '1836 Adieux tempo di Valse', it appears to be an inexact copy of the beginning of **A**1 (see below). 'Adieux' doubtless refers to the fact that Chopin wrote the *Waltz* into Maria Wodzińska's album just before leaving Dresden (see quotations *about the Waltzes...* before the musical text).

A1 Autograph written for Maria Wodzińska, with dedication, signature and date, 'Dresden Sept. 1835' (lost, photocopy at the Fryderyk Chopin Museum, Warsaw). In spite of the haste with which it was written, evident from the character of the script, **A**1 is a very fair copy, with no deletions, and contains a meticulously polished—in musical terms—version of the work, with numerous detailed performance markings. It also contains pencil additions by Chopin, showing that Maria played the *Waltz* from this manuscript under the composer's eye.

A2 Autograph dedicated to Chopin's pupil, Elise Peruzzi, with signature and date, 1837 (Dumbarton Oaks Research Library, Washington DC). In terms of performance markings, **A**2 was elaborated in almost as much detail as **A**1, and the slurring is markedly more mature, more naturally linked to the phrasing. In several places (bars 16, 22 & 48) visible corrections show that minor improvements were made during the writing of **A**2.

A3 Autograph offered to Mlle Charlotte de Rothschild, with dedication, signature and date, 'Paris 1842' (Bibliothèque Nationale, Paris). Written with evident care over the appearance of the notation, it nevertheless contains few performance markings (besides slurring, only *staccato* dots in the R.H. in bars 42-47 and accents in bars 14 & 48). This clearly indicates the occasional, souvenir character of the manuscript. Distinctive is the writing-out in notes of the repeat of bars 17-24.

[**AL**] Lost autograph from which **CL** was made (see below). It presents a version close to the extant autographs, with a few original details.

CL Copy made for Marie Liechtenstein, probably by Fernando da Costa from [**AL**] (Deutsche Bücherei, Leipzig). Above the db^1 in bar 41 & analog. it contains enigmatic signs of unknown provenance. **CL** is written rather carelessly, especially with regard to slurring, yet it is impossible to state whether it corresponds to the notation of [**AL**].

EF Two almost identical posthumous editions, French and German, prepared by Julian Fontana, containing two *Waltzes* (No. 1 *in Ab*, WN 47, No. 2 *in B minor*, WN 19).

FEF Fontana's French edition, J. Meissonnier Fils (J. M. 3526), Paris July 1855. After the fashion of other works edited by Fontana, all the sections which in the manuscripts are marked in short as repeats are written out in **FEF** in notes. It is striking that corresponding bars contain authentic (or very similar) versions appearing in d i f f e r e n t manuscripts (see version of **EF** in the *Appendix*, bars 2-4 & 18-20; 9 & 57; 11, 27 & 123). In general terms the versions of **FEF** can be divided into 3 categories:
— familiar from other sources, of both the original and the later redaction;
— most probably authentic, although not confirmed by the manuscripts—bars 57 & 123 (here and hereafter, numbering of bars according to the version of **FEF** given in the *Appendix*);
— not confirmed by sources, and stylistically more or less dubious (bars 7, 41 & analog., 81-88).
These observations lead to the conclusion that Fontana probably put together versions taken from several different sources, also making arbitrary changes.

GEF Fontana's German edition, A. M. Schlesinger (S. 4395), Berlin July 1855, doubtless based on a proof of **FEF**. In **GEF** the fascicle with these two *Waltzes* was given the inauthentic opus number 69.

Editorial principles
We give two versions of the *Waltz*, based on two autographs musically more meticulously prepared by Chopin (**A**1 & **A**2). We give priority to **A**2, as it is the later version and bears traces of Chopin's work on the text. We cite authentic variants from **A**3, **CL** & **EF**. In the *Appendix* we give the earlier, clearly distinct, redaction and the version of **EF** for which it is difficult to establish the extent of its authenticity (pp. 54-59).

7a. Version in the later autograph. We give the text of **A**2. The variants come from **A**3, **CL** & **EF**. We write out in notes bars 25-40, marked in **A**2 in short as *Dal Segno*. Similarly, bars 57-64 are marked as *Trio da Capo*.
In the further part of this commentary, in addition to discussing editorial problems relating to this version, we signal the more important variants of the text of the *Waltz* in the other sources. (For the identification of the bars discussed, we employ the numbering of the main versions of the *Waltz*; the numbering in the versions given in the *Appendix* is different.)

p. 34 *Bar 1 & analog.* R.H. On the 3rd beat **C**XI, Fr**C**, **CL** & **EF** have even quavers instead of the dotted rhythm.

Bars 2, 4 & analog. L.H. On the 2nd beat **C**XI & Fr**C** have a fourth (the same as on the 3rd beat). This version also appears in **EF**, but only the first time around, in bars 2 & 4.

Bar 3 & analog. R.H. The main text comes from **A**2 & **A**1, the variant from **A**3 & **CL**. In **EF** we encounter both versions: the triplet in bar 3, the grace note in the other bars. This type of alternation can also be found in other works by Chopin, cf. e.g. *Impromptu in F#*, Op. 36, bar 74.

Bars 5, 13 & analog. R.H. In **C**XI & Fr**C** the versions of bars 5 & 13 are differentiated (see *Appendix*, earliest version). In the later redaction Chopin left only the second of the two.

Bars 6-7, 14 & analog. L.H. At the beginning of these bars we give *Eb*, in line with **A**2, **A**1 & **CL**. In the other sources several other versions appear: in **A**3 the octave *Eb-eb* three times, in **C**XI & Fr**C** *eb* three times, in **EF** *eb*, *Eb* and *Eb*. Also different in the last three sources are the chords on the 2nd and 3rd beats.

Bar 7 & analog. R.H. Chopin wrote this bar in different ways:

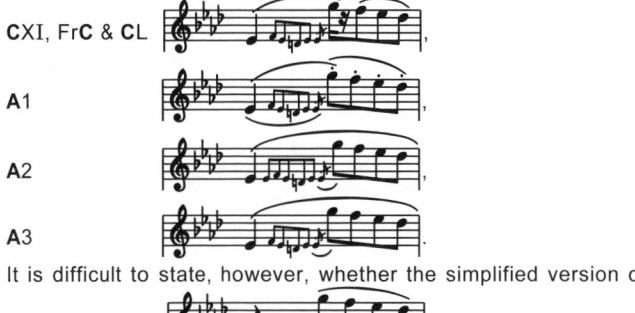

CXI, Fr**C** & **CL**

A1

A2

A3

It is difficult to state, however, whether the simplified version of **EF** is authentic:

Bar 8 & analog. L.H. The ♮ raising the bottom note of the chord on the 3rd beat from *eb* to *e* appears only in **A**2 & **A**3. Cf. a similar transition in the *Waltz in Ab*, WN 28, bars 11-12.

Bar 9 & analog. R.H. At the beginning of the bar **C**XI & Fr**C** have a crotchet db^2 instead of two quavers.

Bar 11 & analog. R.H. The run at the start of the bar has 7 versions in the sources:

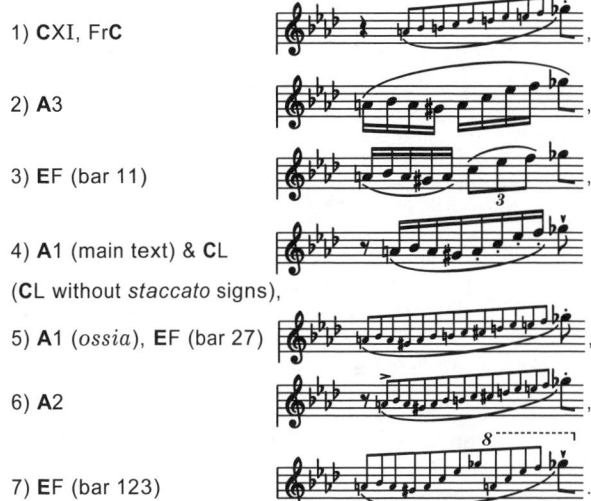

1) **C**XI, Fr**C**

2) **A**3

3) **EF** (bar 11)

4) **A**1 (main text) & **CL**
(**CL** without *staccato* signs),

5) **A**1 (*ossia*), **EF** (bar 27)

6) **A**2

7) **EF** (bar 123)

From the way in which **A**1 is notated, we can infer that Chopin altered version 2, originally written there, to version 4. The *ossia* given in this autograph is the only instance of Chopin thus marking a variant containing a musically different redaction of a particular passage.
We give the version of the basic source (**A**2) and also the most probably authentic version 7, from **EF** (at the last appearance of this phrase). In the latter version we omit the sign ⎯, doubtless an inauthentic addition by Fontana—cf. Chopin's *leggierissimo* in this place in **A**1.

Bar 14 & analog. R.H. **A**1 & **CL** have (different) versions with the chromatic passage through fb^1 (e^1) between the f^1 at the beginning of this bar and the eb^1 in the next. We give the version of **A**2, **A**3 and the other sources.

Bar 15 & analog. R.H. The grace note eb^1 at the beginning of the bar appears only in **A**2.

Bar 16 & analog. R.H. The earlier version (**C**XI & Fr**C**) has the sixth c^1-ab^1 at the beginning of the bar.

Bar 16 R.H. On the 3rd beat the earlier version (**C**XI & Fr**C**) has only the crotchet c^2. Chopin notated the version with two quavers using b^1 (**A**1, **A**3 & **CL**) or cb^2 (**A**2 & **EF**); in **A**2 he deleted b^1 and wrote in cb^2.

Bars 17-24 There are notable differences—above all in rhythm and in the texture of the accompaniment—between the original version (**CXI** & **FrC**, *Appendix*, p. 54) and the other sources. The version of **EF** also departs to some extent from the version of the autographs & **CL**; see version (7b) in the *Appendix*, p. 57, bars 32-48. The rhythmic variant of the 3rd beat of bars 41, 43 & 45 that appears in **EF** is presumably an arbitrary alteration by Fontana.

Bars 18 & 22 L.H. At the beginning of the bar we give the sixth *g-eb^1* that appears in **A2**, **CL** & **EF**. **A1** & **A3** have here the chord *eb-g-eb^1* (as in bar 20). It is worth stressing that in **A2** Chopin deleted the chord in bar 22 and replaced it with the sixth.

Bar 23 R.H. The last two notes are written either as even quavers (**A2** & **A3**, also **EF**, **CXI** & **FrC**) or in the rhythm ♩. ♪ (**A1** & **CL**).

Bar 24 (1ª volta) R.H. The version given by us appears only in **A2**. However, **CXI** & **FrC** also have the same melodic line. L.H. As the 1st note **A1** (alone) has *Eb*, and not *eb*.

Bar 24 (2ª volta) L.H. In **A2** the two *voltas* of bar 24 have an identical accompaniment. A similar pattern appears only in **EF**, but this has the additional note *eb^1* on the 3rd beat. In **A1** & **CL** the 2nd and 3rd beats are the same—*g-bb-eb^1*; this also applies to **A3**—*g-eb^1*.

p. 35 *Bars 41 & 45* L.H. As the 2nd crotchet **A3** has *bb*, as in bars 43 & 47. The lack of differentiation to the accompaniment in these 4 bars also characterises the version of **CXI** & **FrC**, although these sources have here *g*.

Bars 41-48 R.H. The motifs at the transition of bars 41-42 & analog. have a different form in **CXI** & **FrC** (see *Appendix*, p. 55, bar 49 & analog.).

Bar 48 R.H. Chopin introduced the differentiation of the ending of this eight-bar unit (bars 41-48) and its repeats only in **A2** (as a correction during its notation). The original version has a sixth both times, **EF** a third, and the other sources a triad.

Bars 49-56 The rhythmic shifting of the middle eight-bar unit of the *Trio* that appears in **EF** (see *Appendix*, p. 58, bars 80-88) is doubtless an arbitrary alteration by Fontana.
In the original version the sequence of chords has a more schematic form: the L.H. has only octaves and the R.H. only sixths.

Bar 64 R.H. The return of the main part of the *Waltz* (*Da Capo*) is marked in **A1**, **CXI** & **FrC**, and written out in notes in **EF**. Chopin very often notated obvious repeats of this type imprecisely, and so there are no grounds for questioning the use of this same form in the versions of the other sources.

7b. Version in the earlier autograph. We give the text of **A1**, supplemented with variants from **CL** & **A3**.

p. 36 *Bar 7* R.H. This bar contains pencil additions most probably made by Chopin:
— at the beginning of the bar, between the staves *ff* or, more likely, two crosses placed next to one another (a sign that is highly characteristic of Chopin as a teacher, here probably indicating a more difficult place);
— fingering above the top two quavers (*g^2-f^2*), most probably 4 4 (possibly 5 5).
Due to the difficulty with interpreting signs on the black and white photocopy of **A1**, we do not add these to the musical text.

Bar 11 R.H. The *ossia* variant appears with this label in **A1**, written by Chopin on an additional stave above the main text, which is reproduced exactly in our edition. See also note to this bar in version 7a.

Bar 14 & analog. R.H. The main text comes from **A1**, the variant from **CL**.

Bar 24 (2ª volta) L.H. Triads on the 2nd and 3rd beats appear in **A1** & **CL**, sixths in **A3**.

p. 37 *Bar 48* After the 2nd beat **A1** has a double bar-line. Most probably Chopin forgot to add the dots marking a repeat, as his intention to repeat bars 49-64 is attested by the left-hand repeat sign in bar 64, and the repetition of bars 41-48 is marked or written out in all the other sources.

8. Waltz in F minor, WN 55

Of the five extant autographs of this *Waltz* only two are dated. This makes it impossible to establish their chronology and difficult to specify their mutual relations. Statistical analysis of the 46 places in which the autographs differ from one another (discounting slurring and other sporadic performance markings), allows us to draw the following conclusions:
— the autograph offered to Mme Oury contains the elements that form the most stable part of Chopin's conception of this *Waltz*: in 43 of the 46 places analysed, its version is confirmed by at least one other autograph;
— the autograph dedicated to Mlle Gavard contains the greatest number of elements belonging, within this conception, to the area of dynamic changeability: in as many as 21 places it has versions that are different from those of the other autographs;
— the autographs for Mme Oury and Mlle Krudner are the two texts closest to one another, which accords with the difference of barely two days between the dates of their dedications; the second such pair comprises the Rothschilds' autograph and the autograph for Countess Eszterhazy.
A separate case is the version of the *Waltz* contained—with minor discrepancies—in Fontana's copy and edition and in the Wildt edition. This differs considerably from the versions of (all) the autographs, and the authenticity of certain elements raises serious doubts (e.g. the lowered bass line in bars 6-8 or the bass-note extensions in bars 13-17, which give an unplayable span). We may assume that Fontana had at his disposal some working autograph written in short, from which he made several copies, supplementing out of necessity, as he saw fit, places that were difficult or impossible to decipher. The extant fragment would have been one of these copies, while the others could have served as the base text for the above-mentioned editions.

Sources
AR Autograph from the Rothschilds' legacy (Bibliothèque Nationale, Paris). In it, the *Waltz* begins without anacrusis, which may indicate that it is the earliest of the extant autographs.
AE Autograph offered to Countess Eszterhazy, with dedication, Chopin's signature and the expression *legato* at the beginning (Abbaye de Royaumont). It contains pencil additions by Chopin, testifying its use during lessons.
AK Autograph written into the album of Marie de Krudner, with Chopin's dedication and signature, dated 'Paris, 8 December 1842' (the date is sometimes mistakenly read as 8 June 1841; Bibliothèque Nationale, Paris). It is the only autograph with a tempo marking, *All^{to}* [*Allegretto*].
AO Autograph offered to Anne-Caroline de Belleville-Oury, with Chopin's dedication and signature, dated 'Paris, 10 December 1842' (private collection, photocopy at the Fryderyk Chopin Museum, Warsaw).
AG Autograph offered to Elise Gavard, with Chopin's dedication and signature (Bibliothèque Nationale, Paris). The quite numerous corrections testify that Chopin sought to write a well-considered version of the work, and not just offer a fair occasional manuscript.
CX Copy made by an unknown copyist, reproducing, with several errors, the text of **AE** (Bibliothèque Nationale, Paris).

CY Copy of **A**G made by another unknown copyist (Bibliothèque Musicale de l'Opéra, Paris). This very fair, meticulous and faithful copy contains sensible proposals for solutions to several ambiguities in the notation of **A**G (bars 22 & 38 R.H., bar 37 L.H., repeat of the second part).

CC Copy from the legacy of Duchess Marcelina Czartoryska, made—in the opinion of Arthur Hedley—in her own hand (private collection, photocopy at the Fryderyk Chopin Museum, Warsaw). The text of **CC** is closest to that of **AE** (discounting a dozen or so clear errors), yet it also contains a number of elements indicating its provenance from another manuscript (autograph or copy), slightly different to **AE**: performance markings absent from **AE** and a version (original or erroneous) of bars 46-47 convergent with bars 30-31, which may point to the use in the manuscript from which **CC** was made of an abbreviation for bars 37-47.

FC Copy made by Julian Fontana, of which only the second page, from bar 24 to the end, has survived (Biblioteka Publiczna, Bydgoszcz). **FC** displays crucial differences from the autographs (most importantly in bars 25, 27 & analog., 34-35, 50 and 52).

PE First Polish edition, I. Wildt, Kraków 1852, also containing the *Waltz in B minor*, WN 19. According to information given on the cover, both *Waltzes* were written by Chopin, in 1844, into the album of Countess P*** [Plater], which in the case of this *Waltz*—due to a number of places of dubious authenticity—seems very unlikely. Rather, we may presume that the publisher, with a single autograph from the album at his disposal (the *Waltz in B minor*), added a second for marketing purposes, taken from a different, unspecified, source. The text displays only minor deviations from the version of **FC**, yet some of them appear unattributable to possible errors or revisions by the publisher (e.g. in bars 34-35 **PE** has—unlike **FC**—a rhythm convergent with that in the autographs). This suggests that **PE** was prepared from a different manuscript, based on the same source as **FC**. The edition contains several unquestionable errors.

EF Two almost identical posthumous editions, French and German, prepared by Julian Fontana, containing three *Waltzes* (No. 1 *in Gb*, WN 42, No. 2 *in F minor*, WN 55, No. 3 *in Db*, WN 20).

FEF Fontana's French edition, J. Meissonnier Fils (J. M. 3527), Paris July 1855. With regard to pitch and rhythm, the text of **FEF** differs only minimally from the version of **PE**, yet some graphical differences indicate a common source for the two editions rather than a direct dependency. All performance markings in **FEF** were certainly added by Fontana, who was also behind the writing-out in notes of all the repeated fragments.

GEF Fontana's German edition, A. M. Schlesinger (S. 4396), Berlin July 1855, doubtless based on a proof of **FEF**. In **GEF** the fascicle with these three *Waltzes* was given the inauthentic opus number 70.

F = **FC**, **EF** & **PE** (in bars 1-23, **F** = **EF** & **PE**, for lack of those bars in **FC**).

Editorial principles
We give two versions of the *Waltz*, based on **AO** & **AG**. In choosing these autographs, we took into account the following arguments:
— the text of **AO** raises the fewest doubts, as almost all the versions it contains appear in other autographs as well;
— **AG** contains the most performance markings and bears evidence of the fine-tuning of details;
— the texts of these two autographs differ sufficiently clearly that they may be regarded as different versions of the work.
We append to each of the versions, in the form of variants, the musically most significant authentic alternative versions from the other sources.
We give the few dynamic markings, appearing only in **AG**, **AE** & **CC**, in both versions of the *Waltz*. Chopin's fingering comes from **AE**.
We give Fontana's version, edited on the basis of **F**, in the *Appendix* (p. 60-61).

8a. Version in the autograph for Mᵐᵉ Oury. We give the text of **A**O. The variants come from **AK** & **FC**. The performance markings in brackets are taken from **AK**, **AG**, **AE** & **CC**.

In the further part of this commentary, in addition to discussing editorial problems relating to this version, we signal the more important variants of the text of the *Waltz* in the other sources. We do not note the numerous errors of **CC**.

p. 38 *Beginning* R.H. In the sources we encounter the following versions of the beginning (we omit all possible performance markings, except for slurs, ties and accents):

PE does not have the slur, and in **EF** the slur begins from the 1ˢᵗ quaver.
Allegretto appears in **AO** & **AK**, *legato* in **AE** (→**CX**) & **CC**.

Bars 1, 9, 13, 29 & 45 The dynamic markings in brackets come from **CC**.

Bars 1 & 52 The repeat of the whole of the *Waltz* is marked in **FC** & **PE**, and written out in notes in **EF**. Both the actual idea for such a repeat and the link from bar 52 to bar 1 have features of authenticity:
— a similar form was originally displayed by the *Waltz in A minor*, Op. 34 No. 2, as the coda (from the 3ʳᵈ beat of bar 152) was added later; the core of the *Waltz* comprises the once-repeated, musically closed, whole that is formed by bars 17-84;
— the harmonic linking written in the version of the variant of bar 52 appears several times in Chopin's works, cf. *Waltz in Ab*, WN 28, bars 11-12 (musical text and commentary).
See also note to bar 52.

Bar 4 L.H. We give the version of **AO** & **AK**. The other sources do not have the rest on the 3ʳᵈ beat: **AR** & **AE** (→**CX**) have the repeated chord ab-c^1-ab^1, **AG** (→**CY**) has a different version, **F** yet another (see version 8b and *Appendix*).

Bar 5 R.H. The grace note eb^2 appears in **AO**, **AK**, **AR** & **F**; it is absent from **AG** (→**CY**), **AE** (→**CX**) & **CC**.

Bars 5-6 L.H. On the 3ʳᵈ beat **AK** has a rest in bar 5 and the third ab-c^1 in bar 6. We give the convergent version of the other sources. Cf. note to bars 12-13.

Bars 6-8 L.H. The version of **F**, in which the bass descends as far as Bb_1, raises doubts with regard to style: this lowering is continued neither in the subsequent phrase nor anywhere else in the further part of the work. The strengthening or lowering of the bass line was one of most frequent alterations made by Fontana in his editing of the *Oeuvres posthumes*.

Bar 7 L.H. **AG** (→**CY**) has chords in lowered position on the 2ⁿᵈ and 3ʳᵈ beats. An identical chord, but only on the 2ⁿᵈ beat, appears in **F**.

Bar 9 L.H. At the beginning of the bar **AG** (→**CY**) & **AE** (→**CX**) & **CC** have Ab.

Bar 11 R.H. The variant comes from **AK**. This type of varying of a motif through the subdivision of longer values is highly characteristic of Chopin (cf. commentary to the *Mazurka in G minor*, Op. 24 Nº 1 bar 59).

Bar 12 R.H. Only **AO** & **AK** have an ornament at the beginning of the bar.
L.H. As the highest note in the chord on the 2ⁿᵈ beat **AO** & **AK** have f^1; the other sources have d^1.

Bars 12-13 L.H. We give the version of **AO**. In **AK** the rest on the 3rd beat appears in bar 13: . The other sources do not have rests in these bars.

Bars 15-16 R.H. One notes the different version of the melody in **F**. Its authenticity seems unquestionable; cf. a very similar phrase in the only slightly earlier *Sostenuto*, WN 53, bars 19-20. Thus, this may be the first redaction of this fragment.

Bar 18 R.H. The variant comes from **AK** (**AE** also has this version). The other sources have the version with *f#2* which we give in the main text.
L.H. **AG** (→**CY**) has a different version of the accompaniment, and **F** another version again (cf. version 8b and *Appendix*). We give the text of **AO** and the other sources.

Bar 21 L.H. We give the text of **AO**. **AK** has on the 2nd and 3rd beats the seconds *ab-bb* (as in bar 37). The other sources have the triad *f-bb-db1*.

Bar 22 & analog. R.H. On the 1st beat of these bars we give the text of **AO**. Set out below are the melodic figures used in these places in the various sources (*3* = triplet):

	bar 22	30	38	46
AR	*3*	*tr*	⌇	♩
AE	*3*	*tr*	*tr*	⌇
AO	*3*	*tr*	*3*	*tr*
AK	*3*	*tr*	*3*	⌇
AG	♫ or *3*	*3*	♫ or *3*	*3*
F	♫	♫	♫	♫

(The notation of **AG** is not clear; see commentary to version 8b.) In the copies, these versions are simply reproduced (not always accurately).

Bar 22 R.H. On the 3rd beat **AR** has the rhythm ♩. ♩.
L.H. On the 2nd and 3rd beats **AK** has the chords *f-ab-db1*. This version has a rather incidental character, as Chopin did not repeat it in an identical context in bar 38. We give the text of **AO** and the other manuscripts. See musical text and commentary to bars 22 & 38 of the version included in the *Appendix* (pp. 60-61).

p. 39 *Bars 25 & 41* L.H. The accompaniment differs in the sources in both the number of strokes and the arrangement of the chords:

The version adopted by us appears most often, is the simplest and is comfortable to play (the accompaniment does not overlap the R.H. passage).

Bars 26, 34 & 42 R.H. In **AO** the arpeggio at the beginning of the bar appears only in bar 26. In the other sources it appears in other bars as well:

	bar 26	bar 34	bar 42
AR	+	+	-
AE (→**CX**)	+	-	+
AK	-	-	+
AO	+	-	-
AG (→**CY**), **CC**	-	-	-
F	+	+	+

In this situation, it seems appropriate to leave the decision as to whether or not to use an arpeggio in one or more of these places to the performer's discretion.
R.H. The note *db2* is repeated on the 3rd beat in **AK**, **AO** & **F**. In the other sources the minim *db2* at the beginning of the bar is extended with a dot.

Bars 27-29 & 43-45 L.H. The sources differ here in numerous details of the accompaniment. In the particular bars, most of the versions of the sources coincide with at least one of the versions given by us. Separate versions appear only in **AE** (→**CX**) & **CC**: *eb1-ab1* or *c1-eb1-ab1* (notation not clear) as the 2nd beat of bars 27 & 43 and the sixth *eb-c1* as the 2nd and 3rd beats of bars 28 & 44.

Bars 30 & 46 L.H. On the 2nd beat **AG** has *f-ab-db1*. The other sources have—in line with **AO**—the sixth *f-db1* (only in bar 30 in **AR** do we find the triad *f-bb-db1*).

Bar 32 L.H. **AG** is the only source where the harmonic course is varied by a different version of the 3rd beat.

Bar 33 L.H. As in bars 25 & 41, the sources differ with regard to the presence or absence of a stroke on the 2nd beat. The rest appears only in **AO** & **AK** (the latter autograph has the sixth *eb-c1* on the 3rd beat).

Bar 34 R.H. In **AR** the sixth *g1-eb2* that begins the bar is arpeggiated. **F** has an equivalent version with a tied grace note.

Bars 34-35 L.H. The version adopted by us appears in **AO** & **AE** (→**CX**). In **AG** (→**CY**) & **F** the note *g1* appears already on the 2nd beat of bar 34, and in **AR** not until the chords of bar 35. **AK** has in bar 34 the chord *d-g-b* twice.

Bar 35 R.H. At the beginning of the bar **AK** & **F** have the sixth *f1-d2*, in **F** tied over from the sixth in the previous bar. We give the concordant version of the other sources.

Bar 36 R.H. Instead of the rests at the beginning of the bar **AK** & **F** have notes held from the previous bar; **AK** *c2* alone, **F** the whole sixth *eb1-c2*.
L.H. The C minor chord is the foundation of the harmony of this bar in all the sources except **AG**, in which Chopin replaced it with the diminished tetrad *c-a-eb1-gb1-c2*.

Bar 42 R.H. The arpeggio comes from **AK**. Cf. note to bars 26 & 42 of the other version of the *Waltz* (8b).

Bar 50 In **F** this bar is based on a different harmony. Although not confirmed by other sources, this version may be authentic; cf. harmonic variants appearing only in **AG** in bars 32 & 36.

Bar 52 The variant comes from **FC** & **PE**. We omit this version's extension of the 1st note of the L.H. to the value of a minim, as in these sources the too frequent use of this device (see *Appendix*, p. 60-61) is most probably inauthentic. **EF** has a similar version:

The holding of the third *ab-c1* in the L.H. is certainly an addition by Fontana, as the notation of this version would require the marking of the repeat *Dal Segno* in a different place to where it was notated in **FC** & **PE**. It is more than likely, meanwhile, that the holding of *c2* in the R.H. does correspond to Chopin's intentions, as due to the tie in bar 1 even the lack of a tie in bar 52—as it is in **FC** & **PE**—does not preclude such a reading; cf. *Waltz in B minor*, WN 19, beginning (together with commentary) and bars 80-81, and note to *Mazurka in A minor*, WN 60, bar 48.

8b. Version in the autograph for Mlle Gavard. We give the text of **AG**. The variants come from **AK** & **AE**. The performance markings in brackets are taken from **AE** (bars 1 & 20) & **CC** (bars 1, 9, 13, 29 & 45).

p. 40   *Beginning* The expression *legato* comes from **AE** (→**CX**) & **CC**.

Bar 11 R.H. The variant comes from **AK**. This type of varying of a motif through the subdivision of longer values is highly characteristic of Chopin.

Bar 18 R.H. The variant comes from **AE** (**AK** also has this version).

Bar 19 R.H. As the 4th quaver some later collective editions erroneously give c^2.

Bars 20-52 In **AG** the repeat of this segment is imprecisely marked: the sign beginning the repeat is written before the 3rd beat of bar 20, but there is no corresponding sign at the end of the work. **CY** has both repeat signs.

Bars 22 & 38 R.H. The main text and the variant are two ways of deciphering the unclear notation of **AG** in bar 22 (bar 38 is not written out; see note to bar 37): [musical notation]. In **CY** this notation is supplemented in a way that may be considered equivalent to a mordent: [musical notation]. This reading has the advantage that the versions of this bar and of the three bars analogous to it are not identical; this principle is observed in all the other autographs. For this reason, we give a version with mordent, notated in the usual manner, as the main version.

p. 41   *Bars 25 & 41* L.H. In some later collective editions the chords db^1-eb^1-g^1 are erroneously given on the 2nd and 3rd beats.

Bar 37 L.H. In **AG** the L.H. part was not notated in this bar. This may be explained in two ways:
— Chopin regarded this bar as the beginning of the segment written in short as a repeat of bars 21-30, and so he only notated the R.H. part, different to that in bar 21; this leads to the main version, which is a repeat of bar 21;
— Chopin wrote the R.H. part of this bar, marked the next 9 bars in short, with letters from 'a' to 'i', as a repeat of bars 22-30, and forgot about the L.H. part—such as it is in all the other sources; this possibility is included as a variant.

9. Waltz in A minor, WN 63

Sources
AI   Working autograph, without performance markings (Bibliothèque Nationale, Paris). It differs from the later version of the fair autograph in several details of the accompaniment and the rhythm of the melody.
A   Fair autograph, given the title *Walec* (Bibliothèque Nationale, Paris). It formed the basis for all editions of the work, the earliest of which was prepared (together with facsimiles of both autographs) by Suzanne and Denise Chainaye in a special issue of the periodical *La Revue Musicale* (Richard-Masse, Editeurs, Paris 1955).

Editorial principles
We give the text of **A**. We supplement the slurring, not always precisely marked, in accordance with the musical sense and with analogous fragments.

p. 42   *Bar 15* R.H. The trill over the 1st note comes from **AI**. Its absence from **A** most probably results from inattention on Chopin's part, as the following suggests:

— the mordent in a similar melodic context in bar 51;
— the lack of the slurs in bars 9-16, which in **A** fill the second line of music; this testifies a slip in attention by Chopin, who wrote only the notes in this fragment.

APPENDIX

(2a). Waltz in B minor, WN 19
Version in the Polish edition

S o u r c e s —see note to the main versions of the *Waltz*, p. 4.

E d i t o r i a l   p r i n c i p l e s
We give the text of **PE**, compared with the other sources to eliminate probable errors.

p. 46   *Bars 3 & 80* L.H. The notes $c\#^1$ given in brackets may be the result of a misreading of the autograph (see note to version 2a, bars 7, 8 & 40 on p. 9).

Bars 6-7 R.H. The convergent version of all the other sources attests the unquestionable omission from **PE** of the tie sustaining d^3. See also analogous bars 38-39.

Bars 7, 8 & 40 L.H. The notes $c\#^1$ given in brackets may be the result of a misreading of the autograph (see note to these bars in the commentary to version 2a on p. 9).

Bar 16 In **PE** it is not marked how this *Waltz* should end (lack of *Fine*). We suggest ending in bar 16, as in **CZ**.

p. 47   *Bar 34* R.H. In front of the last note **PE** erroneously has a ♯. This is probably an incorrect revision by the publisher.

Bars 36-37 L.H. At the beginning of the bar **PE** erroneously has *d*. With the assumption that in [**A3**] the accompaniment in bar 37 was marked in short as a repeat of bar 36 (as it is in **CY**), this double error seems likely.

p. 48   *Bars 74 & 76* R.H. The lack in **PE** of the natural signs lowering $g\#^2$ to g^2 is most probably the result of an oversight.

Bars 79-80 R.H. As the melodic note is struck at the beginning of bar 80 in none of the other sources, the third $a\#^1$-$c\#^2$ was most probably supposed to have been held over in **PE**.

(2b). Waltz in B minor, WN 19
Version in the edition by J. Fontana

S o u r c e s —see commentary to main versions of the *Waltz*, p. 4.

E d i t o r i a l   p r i n c i p l e s
We give the text of **FEF**.

p. 49   *Bars 13, 15 & analog.* In **GEF** the dynamic markings are missing in these bars.

p. 50   *Bars 40-41* **GEF** has here additionally *rit.* in bar 40 and *tempo* in bar 41.

Bars 56-59 & analog. **GEF** has in these bars neither agogic nor dynamic markings, except for *rit.* in bar 168.

p. 51   *Bars 94-95* Instead of *rit.* in bar 95 **GEF** has *riten.* in bar 94.

Bar 97 **GEF** has here additionally   .

(7a). Waltz in A flat major, WN 47
Earliest version

S o u r c e s—see commentary to main versions of the *Waltz*, p. 12.

Editorial principles
We give the text of **FrC** compared with **C**XI.

p. 54   *Bars 7, 15 & analog.* R.H. In **C**XI the small notes are joined with a semiquaver beam.

Bars 11 & 43 L.H. The notes *a* on the 2nd and 3rd beats appear in **FrC**, but not in **C**XI.
R.H. On the 3rd beat **C**XI has the rhythm ♪ ♩.

Bars 15 & 47 L.H. The notes *eb* on the 2nd and 3rd beats of bar 15 appear in **FrC**, but not in **C**XI. In bar 47 **FrCII** & **C**XI have the same text as in bar 15. **FrCI** has a most probably erroneous version—see note to bars 47-48.

Bars 16 & 48 We give *Fine* in bar 16, as given in **C**XI. In **FrC** this expression appears in bar 48, which is unlikely to correspond to Chopin's intentions (see main versions of the *Waltz* and remarks on form in the commentary to the earlier version of the *Waltz in B minor*, WN 19).

Bar 17 & analog. R.H. At the end of these bars **C**XI has the rhythm ♩. ♪.

Bar 24 L.H. At the end of the bar **C**XI has the crotchet *bb*, as in the previous bars.

p. 55   *Bars 47-48* L.H. In the whole of bar 47 and on the 1st and 2nd beats of bar 48 **FrCI** has a text like that in bars 7-8 (39-40). The unquestionable error of the copyist is testified by **FrCII**, which has the version of bars 15-16, in line with **C**XI.

Bars 49-56 L.H. We give the more exact performance markings of **C**XI. **FrC** has only *stringendo* in bars 49-50 and a pause in bar 56.

Bars 56 & 72 L.H. We give the version of **FrC**. **C**XI has a minim *Ab* instead of the first 2 crotchets.

(7b). Waltz in A flat major, WN 47
Version in the Fontana edition

S o u r c e s—see commentary to main versions of the *Waltz*, p. 12.

Editorial principles
We give the text of **E**F.

(8). Waltz in F minor, WN 55
Version in the Polish edition and Fontana's copy

S o u r c e s – see commentary to main versions of the *Waltz*, p. 14.

Editorial principles
We give the text of **F**C. In places where **F**C or **E**F have versions confirmed by the autographs, these are given instead of the versions of **PE**, which in this situation are certainly inauthentic. In keeping with **F**C & **P**E we give no performance markings. (The extant fragment of **F**C begins in bar 24.)

p. 60   *Beginning* R.H. The tie sustaining *c²* appears only in **E**F.

Bars 12-17 and 21-24 & analog. L.H. We adopt the simplified graphical notation of these bars that appears in **F**C and in most places in **E**F. In **P**E rests were added above the minims, and the chords were notated with stems pointing up.

Bar 20 (1ᵃ volta) R.H. In **PE** & **EF** the minim *eb¹* also has a dot extending its value, which is an obvious error given the *e¹* in the chord on the 3rd crotchet of the L.H.

Bars 21-24 & analog. and 49-52 (1ᵃ volta) L.H. The sources differ in the values of the first, extended, note. **F**C has only minims, while **PE** & **EF** generally have dotted minims:
— in **PE** undotted minims appear only in bars 31 & 45;
— in **EF**, in which the repeat of the whole of the *Waltz*, marked *Dal Segno*, is written out in notes, undotted minims appear in bars 40 & 45-47 the first time around, and in bars 24, 29-31 & 45 in the repeat.
Guided by harmonic considerations, we adopt normal minims in bars 30, 46 & 52 (1ᵃ volta), and dotted minims in the remainder.

Bars 22 & 38 L.H. In both bars we give the version which **F**C has in bar 38. **EF** & **PE** have on the 3rd beat the chord *eb-g-db¹*, which is certainly an arbitrary alteration (by analogy with bars 30 & 46, unjustified given the different harmonic sequence).

p. 61   *Bars 24 & 40* L.H. The note *c¹* on the 2nd beat appears in **FC** & **PE** in both these bars, and in **EF** only in bar 40. As the discrepancy among sources suggests a possible error, we treat this note as optional in both bars (cf. similar bars 32 & 48).

Bars 27 & 43 R.H. Missing before the 1st third on the 2nd beat in **FC** & **PE** is the ♮ raising *bb¹* to *b¹*.

Bar 33 R.H. As the last note **PE** has *d²*, quite clearly by error.

Bar 34 L.H. In both chords **PE** additionally has the erroneous note *eb¹*.

Bars 35-36 R.H. In both bars **F**C has the rhythm | ♩. ♪♩ |.

Bar 50 R.H. Missing in **F**C is the ♮ raising *eb¹* to *e¹*.

Bar 52 (1ᵃ volta) We give the version of **FC** & **PE**. The tie sustaining *c²* appears only in **EF**. See note to this bar in version 8a.

Works lost, inaccessible and dubious

The list compiled by Ludwika Jędrzejewicz (see characterisation of **IJ** in the commentary to the *Waltz in E*, WN 18) includes the incipits of six waltzes which would have been included in the present volume were it not for their incomplete form. We list them here with all the notes that concern them.

Waltz in C. '1824 Date uncertain, among the earlier works':

(In spite of a number of doubts, we leave the notation without corrections, as it is difficult to indicate where the errors occur and how to correct them.)

Waltz in C. '1826':

(We correct the obvious errors: metre from 3/4 to 3/8 and bottom note of the chords in bars 1-3 from *e* to *g*.)

Waltz in Ab. '1827 Valse':

(The rhythmic value of the anacrusis is not certain: a quaver *eb¹* is written in the R.H. above the crotchet rest in the L.H.; we give a more likely version with crotchet.)

Waltz in D minor. '1828 Valse la partenza':

The title *la partenza* (the departure) is possibly linked to one of Chopin's journeys of that year: in the summer to Sanniki or in September to Berlin.

Waltz in Ab. '1829 Valse v[el] 30':

(We correct the erroneous time signature from 3/4 to 3/8.)

Waltz in Eb. 'Valse 1829 v[el] 30':

(In bar 3 we correct the most probably erroneous 1st quaver of the lower voice of the R.H. from *g¹* to *ab¹*.)

There also possibly exists a *Waltz in B*, the autograph of which Chopin presented to Madame Erskine on 12 Oct. 1848 (name and date on the title page, written in Chopin's hand). However, the manuscript is held in an inaccessible private collection and at the present time its contents cannot be verified.

A *Waltz in Eb*, with the character of a ländler, that is ascribed to Chopin, published by Breitkopf & Härtel (ed. Ferdynand Hoesick) together with the *Waltz in Ab*, WN 28 (see commentary),

displays too few features of Chopin's music to be considered authentic. This judgment is not undermined by the testimony of Hoesick, who considered the manuscript of this work contained in the album of Emilia Elsner to be a Chopin autograph, as this distinguished Chopin biographer was not immune from mistakes in identifying the composer's script. Hence this work is not included in our edition.

Jan Ekier
Paweł Kamiński